Incentive Compensation Strategies for the New Millennium

Incentive Compensation Strategies for the New Millennium

A Practical Guide on How to Successfully Design, Implement and Manage Employee Incentive Programs

Rami R. Loya

Bulk Purchase
This book is available at a special discount when ordered in large quantities.
For details and discount information please contact:

IncenSoft LLC
951-C Russell Ave.
Gaithersburg, MD 20879
Tel: 1-888-393-3255
Email: sales@incensoft.com

ISBN: 0-9679891-0-8

To my wife, Michelle

*Whose encouragement, dedication, and support
made this book possible.*

Acknowledgments

I owe my sincere appreciation to several individuals who were instrumental in bringing this book to reality.

Paty Nieto, my loyal "right-hand," who spent endless hours, with great patience and diligence, helping me put this book together.

Ken Clark, my talented graphic designer, whose inspiring ideas created the book's cover. Ken also spent many hours helping me create the earlier version of this publication.

My friend and colleague Don Tabasco, whose energetic personality and drive encouraged me along the way.

Patricia Young, my editor, whose fresh eye and perspective helped put the finishing touches on this book.

Ren Nardoni, whose valuable input, support, and guidance contributed to focusing this book on its targeted audience.

Should I have overlooked anyone, please accept my apologies in advance.

TABLE OF CONTENTS

CHAPTER FOUR...41

PERFORMANCE EVALUATION AND PERSONAL OBJECTIVES

CHAPTER FIVE..51

PLAN IMPLEMENTATION, ADMINISTRATION, AND MONITORING

CHAPTER SIX...59

THE SURVEY PROCESS

CHAPTER SEVEN..87

INCENTIVE PLAN IN ACTION

INTRODUCTION

In the highly competitive business environment of the new millennium, companies are continually looking for ways to maintain leadership, get ahead of competitors, and develop innovative products and services that will set them apart.

It has been concluded that an organization's most valuable asset is its human resource, most recently referred to as "Human Capital." With human capital, an organization can become whatever it aspires to be. Without human capital, an organization cannot exist. Employees are the most important factor in organizational success and survival. However, the question remains, how to unify this group of people under a common goal and stimulate their creativity, self-sufficiency, and productivity?

Successful and innovative technological advancements are the direct result of focusing individuals in group settings to delve into their innermost ability and create something that no one else has done in the past. Barriers are tossed aside, challenging goals are established, and everyone rolls up his sleeves to get the job done.

This is how Lee Iacoca created the new Chrysler Corporation and how Bill Gates made Microsoft Corporation a world leader in computer software. There are more examples of innovation and success. One thing is clear; none of these companies would have succeeded without a hardworking, dedicated, and motivated work force striving to reach for the ultimate goal of excellence.

This book serves as a practical guide on successfully designing and implementing incentive compensation programs in most organizations. Such programs will facilitate the motivational forces and reward tools necessary to drive the organization's performance to new levels. Also, this book incorporates the tools required to manage, administer, and monitor incentive compensation programs in the workplace.

CHAPTER ONE
HOW TO DRIVE THE PERFORMANCE OF YOUR BUSINESS

1.1 The Business Performance Model

Facilitating Business Performance is a simple and rewarding management decision. Business owners and executives, who want to grow their revenue and earnings, must first put in place the tools to allow the organization to reach its maximum potential.

Figure 1.1 on *page 4* is a flowchart of a Business Performance Model, which describes the critical elements needed in order to obtain successful results. These elements and the theories behind them are explained in detail in Chapter 11.

Motivation is the driving force behind performance. Motivated employees tend to reach their full potential and encourage colleagues with their enthusiasm and passion to elevate their performance and reach new heights.

In the same way, people who perform well expect to be rewarded fairly for their efforts. Equitable rewards foster job satisfaction and high morale. Motivated and happy employees are loyal to their employer and are likely to remain committed to the company. They will encourage others to join their organization and possibly attract new talent.

With equitably rewarded performance, workforce productivity tends to rise and business efficiency improves. Productivity and efficiency facilitate growth in revenue and earnings, allowing the company to continue rewarding good performance. This value creation cycle re-energizes itself as long as the motivational forces are continually present.

Lack of motivation and/or rewards will yield the exact opposite effect: an unmotivated, unhappy, and non-productive workforce that can have a devastating affect on the long-term survival of an organization.

Figure 1.1

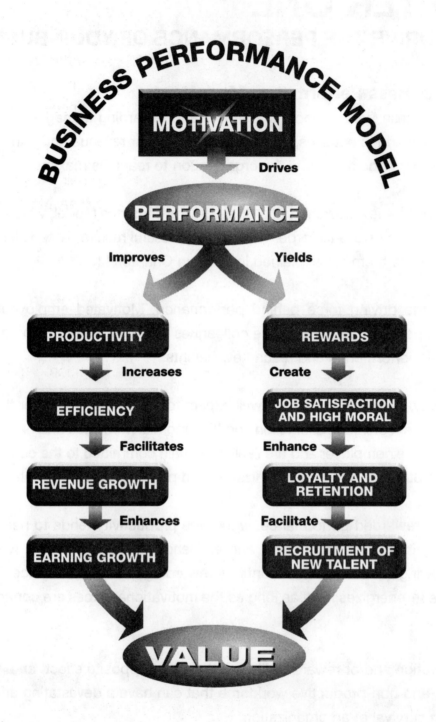

1.2 What is Human Capital?

Human capital is defined as the combined sum of knowledge, intellectual capacity, skills, resources, experiences, and goodwill existing within the workforce of an organization. Human capital cannot be duplicated easily by other companies; therefore, it can become a source of ***sustainable competitive advantage***. This capital is acquired by individuals through education, training, research, and experiences in their professional career.

The greater human capital an individual possesses, the higher their income level. The risk to companies is that the human capital they employ is increasingly mobile and constantly subjected to tempting opportunities and offers from other sources. When individuals leave organizations, their knowledge goes with them and the cost to replace that knowledge is extremely high. Companies have to develop innovative strategies to ***retain and preserve this invaluable resource***.

1.3 The Human Capital Formula

Human capital has recently surfaced to the highest level of attention in the corporate world. It has been referred to as the most valuable asset in organizational success and prosperity.

With shrinking labor markets and a highly competitive recruiting environment created by the Internet technology revolution, human capital is the most critical factor in an organization's ability to compete effectively in the new millennium.

How can organizations appraise or assess the value of this tremendous resource? We believe that the following formula defines it best:

$$HC = (M) \times (P) \times (R)$$

Where:

HC	=	Human Capital
M	=	Motivation
P	=	Performance
R	=	Rewards

- Motivation is the basic element to drive the performance of the workforce.
- Performance builds and accelerates the value of the enterprise.
- Rewards continue to energize motivation and performance.

Without the presence of these three elements, the value of human capital will deteriorate and diminish over time.

1.4 How Motivation and Rewards Drive the Value of the Business

From reviewing the human capital formula, we notice the multiplication signs between the three components:

Human Capital   =   Motivation   X   Performance   X   Rewards

In order to optimize the value of human capital, all three elements must be present and must be utilized to their fullest extent for each person in the organization. By maximizing human capital, companies will increase the value of their corporate assets and optimize the return on the investment they are making in developing their human capital. Motivation drives performance; performance yields rewards; and rewards re-fuel and re-ignite motivation to keep it going… and going… and going.

Figure 1.4   The Value Creation Cycle

1.5 The Program that Forces You to Manage Your Business Effectively

In today's hectic business environment, too many executives are busy juggling daily schedules and putting out fires. Most know in the back of their minds that there are better ways to manage and that there are good solutions to the problems brushed aside due to lack of time. In the end, these problems become the fires that they have to deal with every day.

"Pay now or pay later" is the familiar quote. Ignoring problems doesn't make them go away and, in most cases, the price tag to fix them later is generally high. The program developed in this book, if followed, *will force companies to plan and manage their businesses effectively.*

Managing effectively is accomplished by mandating the following activities:
- Creating a long-term strategic plan for the company
- Setting short-term and long-term goals for the company
- Focusing each employee on core competencies and personal goals
- Providing clear definition of the performance criteria
- Providing clear definition of rewards that are performance-contingent
- Continually measuring performance and goal attainment
- Rewarding the workforce equitably for achievements
- Monitoring progress
- Revising the program as needed

1.6 Objectives of this Book

This book is a practical approach to creating incentive compensation plans to motivate employees and enhance productivity in the workplace. It details the methods of designing such plans and provides step-by-step instructions on how to effectively implement and manage incentive compensation plans in most organizations.

Samples of actual plans, illustrations, tables, and flowcharts with live examples will demonstrate how flexible plans tailored for each organization can be put in place quickly and cost-effectively. Several categories in which employees such as technology, manufacturing, engineering, sales, procurement, quality, executives, etc., can be incorporated.

This book is printed in large and clear letters for easy reading and key points and terminologies are highlighted.

1.7 Who Should Use It

Management of any business or company seeking more effective ways to create a *self-motivated, productive, and loyal work force* to maintain their competitive edge, improve earnings, and ensure the long term success of their organization.
This includes:

- Business executives – Chairman, CEO, President, COO, CFO, Exec. VP, etc.
- Human resource executives and managers – VP of Human Resources, HR Director, HR Manager, etc.
- Compensation Directors and Managers
- Entrepreneurs – From start-up to well-established stages
- Employee Benefit Managers
- Sales and Marketing Executives
- Business Owners/Operators

The incentive compensation program described in this book can be applied to a whole company or to any independent business unit, division, or subsidiary operated by a parent company.

1.8 Why Should You Motivate your Employees

- Increase profitability
- Increase productivity and efficiency
- Create a self-motivated performance-driven workforce
- Increase the value of human capital
- Increase shareholder value
- Improve job satisfaction
- Improve morale in the workplace
- Improve employee loyalty
- Reduce turnover
- Attract new talent
- Unite all employees under common goals
- Ensure the long-term success of your business

1.9 What Should You do Before You Start

- Read this book thoroughly.
- Convince yourself that this program is in the best interest of your company or business.
- Use this book (and optional software) to design a hypothetical plan for your company with real-life examples.
- Present your plan to decision-making executive(s) in a convincing manner—emphasize advantages.
- Get executive's *long-term commitment, involvement,* and *support* to implementing the plan.
- Establish a timetable for implementation.

1.10 How to Convince Your Management

- Prepare a convincing presentation using the plan you designed from this book (and optional software).
- Demonstrate the plan in motion based on assumptions you made. Show examples in real time of how the plan would work should it be approved.
- Demonstrate the long-term benefits to the company.
- Emphasize that the plan is flexible, it can be adjusted, modified, or changed as needed.

Figure 1.10 on *page 11* is a flowchart of how to convince your management to adopt an incentive compensation program.

Fig. 1.10   How to Convince your Management

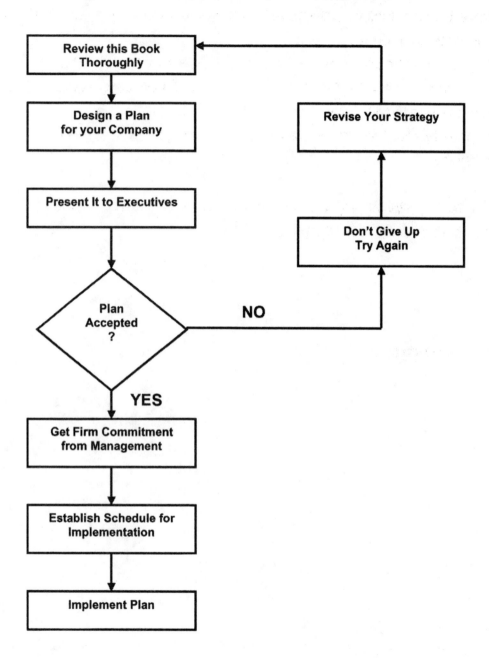

CHAPTER TWO
HOW TO SETUP AND IMPLEMENT AN INCENTIVE PLAN

2.1 Introduction

The focus of this chapter is to guide you through the steps in implementing an incentive compensation plan, which will be directly linked to the business goals and the financial performance of the corporation. This plan is intended to supplement and complement existing plans such as profit sharing, 401(k), stock options, stock purchase, etc., and not to replace them. It will convey a clear and simple message to all employees:

No Financial Gain = No Incentive Payments

Increased Financial Gain = Increased Incentive Payments

2.2 Incentive Compensation Plan Implementation

Figure 2.2 on *page 15* is a flowchart of the steps in implementing an incentive compensation plan. Each step is explained in detail in this book.

2.3 Setting the Corporate Goals

The first step in creating an incentive plan is to set the long-term (three to five years) strategic corporate goals for the company. An example of such goals is shown in Table 2.3 on *page 14*. These goals should reflect the company's aspirations and long term strategic plans. Management should review its strategic plan and set the goals for its employees on a yearly basis. Goals must be *realistic and attainable* for employees to believe that they can achieve the targets successfully. The goals have to be *well communicated to all employees* at the beginning of the company's fiscal year (or at the plan kick-off stage) in order to allow employees to put forth the effort in meeting these goals. *Employees who are not aware of the corporate goals can't help the company reach them.*

Table 2.3   Corporation Three Year Goals

CORPORATE GOALS	2000	2001	2002
SALES	10,000,000	20,000,000	40,000,000
PROFIT BEFORE TAXES	750,000	1,800,000	4,000,000
STOCKHOLDER EQUITY	1,000,000	2,000,000	4,400,000
GROSS PROFIT MARGIN (GPM)	36%	37%	38%
NEW PRODUCT DEVELOPMENT	2	4	6
INCREASE MARKET SHARE	16%	20%	25%
INCREASE CUSTOMER SATISFACTION	95%	96%	97%
SHARE VALUE OF STOCK	$6.00	$9.00	$13.50
YEAR 2003 PUBLIC OFFERING			

2.4 Setting the Organizational Structure

The second step is to setup the organization's structure (if not in place yet). The organizational structure must be analyzed for the purpose of dividing and arranging the workforce into the main groups, subgroups, teams, etc., that will participate in the incentive compensation plan. This step is needed in order to focus each segment of the company on its specific corporate goals.

Groups should be functional units, which are subject to similar work conditions or job function. Subgroups may be individuals (i.e. Director of Marketing) or several employees performing a very similar job (i.e. QC Inspectors).

Figure 2.4 and Table 2.4 on *page 16* demonstrate how an organizational chart is translated into a table format that organizes the company into groups, subgroups, work teams, etc.

Fig. 2.2 Steps in the Implementation of an Incentive Compensation Plan

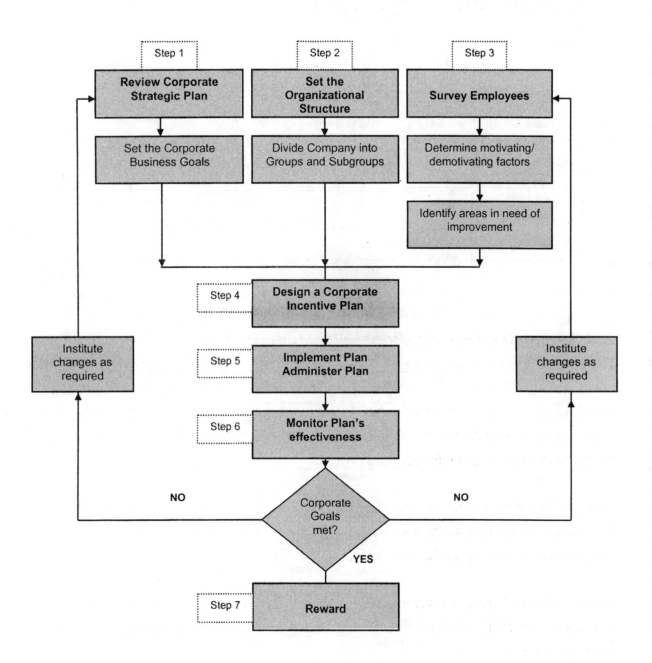

Fig. 2.4 Organizational Structure

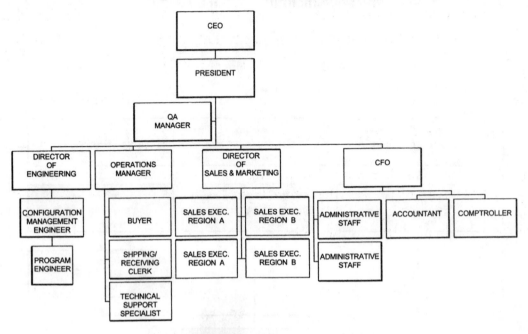

Table 2.4 Groups, Subgroups, Teams

Group	Subgroup	Team	# of Employees
Executive (3)	CEO		1
	President		1
	QA Manager		1
Engineering (3)	Director of Engineering		1
	Configuration Mgmt Engineer		1
	Program Engineer		1
Operations (4)	Operation Manager		1
	Technical Support Specialist		1
	Shipping/Receiving Clerk		1
	Buyer		1
Sales and Marketing (5)	Director of Sales and Marketing		1
	Sales Executives	Sales Exec. Region A	2
		Sales Exec. Region B	2
Finance / Administration (5)	CFO		1
	Accountant		1
	Comptroller		1
	Admin. Staff		2
		Total Employees	**20**

2.5 Surveying Employees

The third step in implementing the incentive plan is to conduct an employee survey that will provide insightful feedback to management as to what areas within the organization are lacking attention and what is important for the company's success from the employees' point of view.

The purpose of the survey is:

a) To determine the motivating and de-motivating factors affecting the performance of the company's workforce.

b) To provide an indication of satisfaction and morale levels amongst employees, and

c) Highlight areas where the company needs to improve its service and support to its employees so they can perform their jobs effectively.

The survey has to be performed in a confidential manner and its results are to be compiled by the Human Resources department or an independent party outside the organization. It is preferred to have the survey conducted by an outside firm specializing in surveys and polling. Questions and ratings method used in the survey need to be explained **to all employees in detail** to avoid mis-understandings and to maximize the accuracy of the survey.

The organizational structure established in Step 2.4 is used for surveying the employees. Employees will be surveyed by functional groups. Group surveys will be structured to answer questions about the corporation in general and about areas related to the specific needs of each group.

It is critical to have a high participation level in the survey for it to be meaningful and productive. To stimulate high participation each participant can be presented with a gift such as a mug, T-shirt or other promotional item when the survey is completed. The survey results need to be analyzed carefully in order to determine motivational and demotivational factors, morale level and areas in need of improvement. The details of the survey process, how to conduct it, analyze its results, and provide management with conclusions and recommendations are covered thoroughly in Chapter 6.

Steps 4 through 7 in the implementation process of incentive compensation plans will be described in detail in the following chapters:

- Step 4 - Design of an Incentive Plan is described in Chapter 3
- Steps 5 and 6 - Plan Implementation, Administration and Monitoring are described in Chapter 5.
- Step 7 - How to Reward the Workforce, is described in Chapter 9.

2.6 15 Rules for Successful Implementation of an Incentive Compensation Plan

1. Link employee goals to your business plan.
2. Set realistic and attainable goals.
3. Conduct an employee survey.
4. Identify areas where company needs to improve its service and support levels for all employees.
5. Define the performance criteria clearly.
6. Identify motivational rewards that will have a positive impact on the work behavior of employees.
7. Link rewards to financial performance of the company.
8. Minimize subjective performance evaluation criteria.
9. Involve employees and managers in the planning stages of the program.
10. Rally employees and managers to buy into the plan.
11. Communicate the plan and its progress to all the employees throughout all stages.
12. Automate plan to minimize the administrative burden.
13. Provide employees with access to their goal/reward data and progress toward goal attainment (intranet/Internet).

14. Reward in a timely manner.
15. Monitor the plan progress periodically and make improvements or changes as required.

CHAPTER THREE
HOW TO DESIGN AN INCENTIVE COMPENSATION PLAN

3.1 Plan Principles

The purpose of the plan is to provide employees with a periodic (monthly, quarterly, etc.) incentive pay based on three key factors:

      1. **Company's Profitability**
      2. **Meeting Corporate Goals**
      3. **Individual's Performance**

The plan will operate on the following principles:

(i) Set the Goals

The Company will set the corporate and individual's goals on an annual basis and revise them during the year as necessary.

(ii) Measure Performance

The company will measure its performance and the performance of the individuals on the plan at predetermined intervals.

(iii) Reward

The company will reward the employees depending on the measured results at the end of each interval.

3.2 Plan Structure

- The plan is based on several **incentive factors** (business goals), which have been determined critical to the company's success.

- Employees are divided into **functional groups** and **subgroups** according to the organization's structure.

- Each employee group is compared to the incentive factors and their potential influence and impact on these factors is determined. Each group is then assigned to the incentive factors they have responsibility for and control over. Not all the incentive factors are assigned to every group.

- Each subgroup is examined with regard to the incentive factors selected for that group and is assigned the factors on which they are to focus their efforts. A weight is allocated to each incentive factor selected for the subgroup. The **factor weight** indicates the importance and priority each factor plays within the subgroup in relation to reaching its goals. The total percentage allocated for all incentive factors per subgroup should be 100 percent.

- Generally, it is recommended to assign not more than four incentive factors per subgroup and not less than 10 percent weight for any factor selected. Factors with weights of less than 10 percent will become negligible in the total incentive picture and are likely to be ignored.

3.3 Incentive Plan Design Flowchart

Figure 3.3 on *page 23* depicts a flowchart of the 10 steps in designing an incentive compensation plan. Each step is explained in detail in this chapter.

3.4 *Step One* – Determining Incentive Factors

The first step in the design of an incentive plan is to determine the incentive factors, generally referred to as business goals.

3.4.1 What are Incentive Factors

Incentive factors are elements through which the organization can achieve its long-term strategic goals. They are critical to the lasting success and survival of the organization and are essential for maintaining the organization's value, growth, image, reputation, quality standards, customer service, and public relations.

Fig. 3.3 10 Steps in the Design of an Incentive Compensation Plan

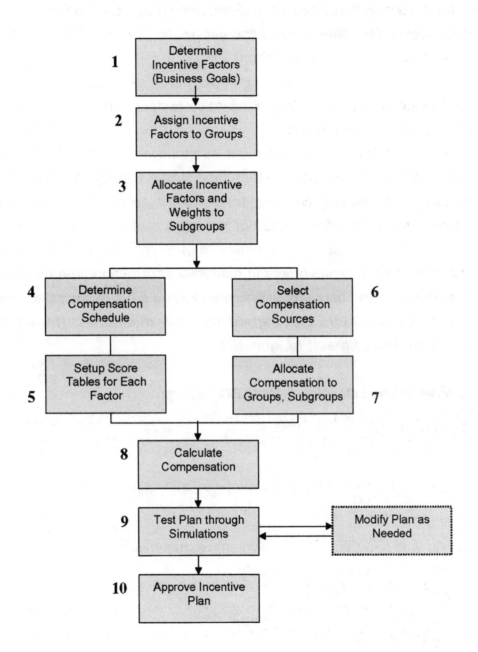

Incentive factors are established in coordination with the corporate strategic goals (See Chapter 2, section 2.3). They are the ***driving forces that motivate and encourage employees to reach and exceed the set goals***.

Incentive factors vary from company to company and from industry to industry. Each company has to select its own unique incentive factors carefully since they are the foundation of the incentive program.

Incentive factors must be measurable by a quantitative method. Such measurements are to be ***internally generated*** by the company for the period the bonus is being paid. For example, if you select a factor stating, "Increase customer satisfaction to 98 percent," the organization must have an established method to record customer complaints and measure the improvement in customer satisfaction. The financial department of the company can generate financial and sales data used by the plan.
Do not use incentive factors that cannot be easily measured. It will complicate your plan and make it difficult to administer.

Listed below are some examples of incentive factors:

- Achieving Corporate Sales Goals
- Improving Gross Profit Margin
- Booking New Sales Orders
- Cost Reduction Efforts
- Controlling Budget
- Complying with ISO 9001 Quality System Requirements
- Accelerating Product Development Cycle
- Improving Customer Satisfaction
- Improving Efficiency of Manufacturing Process
- Increasing Production Yield
- Reducing Production Scrap
- Controlling Expenses
- Increasing Market Share
- Increasing Inventory Turnover Cycle

- Improving Account Receivable Collection Cycle
- Personal Performance Evaluation
- Personal Objectives

3.4.2 Calculation Methods for Incentive Factors

Several calculation methods can be used to measure the progress of attaining incentive factor goals.

1) Percent

This method is used for factors that are measured as a straight percent, for example,

- Return on investment = 25%
- Return on capital = 22%

This calculation method is based on the range of variation in percentage that a factor can change, i.e. gross profit margin can vary from 25 to 40 percent. In this method, achieving higher percentages will lead to higher incentive pay.

2) Percent of Goal Achieved

This method is based on what percentage of the goal has been achieved. For example, if the sales goal was $1M and the actual sales were $ 900,000, the percent of goal achieved is,

$$\frac{900,000}{1,000,000} = 90\%$$

In this method, the higher percentage of goal achieved, the higher incentive is paid.

3) Percent Decrease from Goal

This calculation is based on how many percentage points were below the goal. For example, if a budget was set for $100,000/period and actual expenditures were $95,000, the percent by which the budget is below target:

$$\frac{100,000 - 95,000}{100,000} = 5\%$$

This method rewards achieving targets below the set benchmark because it rep-resents additional savings to the organization.

4) Units

This calculation method is based on variation in number of units from goal. For example, if production goal was 1,000 units per period and 1,050 units were produced, the goal was exceeded by 50 units. This method rewards achieving higher unit measures than the set goal.

5) Units Above Goal

This calculation method is based on how many units were produced above the goal level. This is used to drive the number of units upwards.

6) Units Under Goal

This calculation method can be used to reward employees based on how many units were used below normal useage. For example, if normal use is 100 boxes of paper per period and employess reduce consumption to 90 boxes – cutting expenses – this calculation method may be used.

7) Percent of Unit Goal Achieved

This calculation method is based on the percentage of actual units measured in respect to the goal. For example, if the goal was to produce 100 units and 110 were produced, percentage of unit goal achieved is:

$$\frac{110}{100} = 110\%$$

3.5 *Step Two* – Assigning Incentive Factors to Groups

Incentive factors are assigned to the groups that have responsibility, influence and/or control over them. Not all incentive factors apply to every group, but a few apply to each group. Employees should constantly review the incentive factors and goals assigned to them, monitor their progress, and adjust their priorities and emphasis toward reaching them. The incentive factors and goals serve as constant reminders to employees as to which areas their efforts should be focused.

The following table shows an example of the distribution of eight incentive factors among five employee groups.

Table 3.5 Incentive Factors for Company ABC

Incentive Factors	Groups				
	Executive	Engineering	Operations	Sales	Administration
Sales (Dollars)	✓	✓	✓	✓	✓
GPM (%)	✓		✓	✓	✓
Cost Reduction	✓		✓		✓
Product Development	✓	✓			
Budget	✓	✓	✓		✓
Customer Satisfaction	✓	✓		✓	✓
Performance Evaluation			✓		✓
Personal Objectives		✓	✓		✓

3.6 *Step Three* – Allocating Incentive Factors and Weights to Subgroups

Once the incentive factors have been identified and assigned to each group, the subgroups within each group are examined carefully to determine on which factors they should focus. For example, a group may have been assigned six factors, but the subgroup level will be assigned only the three factors on which they need to concentrate.

Next, a weight is distributed among the factors assigned to each subgroup based on the importance each factor plays within the subgroup in relation to reaching the set

Table 3.6 Factor Weight Distribution at the Subgroup Level

Factor Weight Distribution by Subgroup

Group	Subgroup	Sales	GPM	Cost Reduct.	Product Develop.	Budget	Cust. Satisf.	Employ. Evaluat.	Personal Objectv.	Total Weight
Executive (3)	CEO	30	20	10	15	10	15	--	--	100%
	President	40	20	--	20	--	20	--	--	100%
	QA Manager	25	--	25	25	--	25	--	--	100%
Engineering (3)	Director of Engineering	30	--	--	50	10	10	--	--	100%
	Configuration Mgmt Engineer	25	--	--	45	10	10	--	10	100%
	Program Engineer	30	--	--	50	10	--	--	10	100%
Operations (4)	Operations Manager	25	25	25	--	25	--	--	--	100%
	Technical Support Specialist	30	15	25	--	15	--	15	--	100%
	Shipping/Receiving Clerk	50	--	20	--	--	--	15	15	100%
	Buyer	--	25	50	--	--	--	--	25	100%
Sales and Marketing (5)	Director, Sales and Marketing	50	35	--	--	--	15	--	--	100%
	Sales Exec. Region A	60	30	--	--	--	10	--	--	100%
	Sales Exec. Region B	60	30	--	--	--	10	--	--	100%
Finance / Admin. (5)	CFO	25	25	25	--	25	--	--	--	100%
	Accountant	--	--	30	--	30	10	10	20	100%
	Comptroller	--	--	30	--	30	10	10	20	100%
	Administrative Staff	--	--	20	--	20	10	20	30	100%

goals. The factor weight is the percentage of the factor allocated to a specific subgroup. The total factor weight for each subgroup should equal 100 percent. Weight is allocated only to the incentive factors selected for the subgroup. Avoid allocating weights of less than 10 percent per factor.

Group directors and managers should be involved and play an active role in allocating incentive factors to subgroups and in deciding their weights.

Table 3.6 on *page 28* demonstrates an example of the weight distribution for incentive factors at the subgroup level.

3.7 *Step Four* – Determining Compensation Schedule

The compensation schedule is the period during which progress toward achieving the goal is measured and incentive payment is calculated. At the end of the compensation period, comparing the incentive factor goals to the actual performance results will determine the compensation pay for the groups and subgroups. Compensation schedules may be bi-weekly, monthly, quarterly, semi-annually or annually. Table 3.7 is an example of a compensation schedule:

Table 3.7   Compensation Schedule for Each Group

	Compensation Schedule			
Groups	**Monthly**	**Quarterly**	**Semi-annually**	**Annually**
Executive			✓	
Engineering		✓		
Operations		✓		
Sales & Marketing	✓			
Finance/Admin.		✓		

3.8 *Step Five* – Setting up Score Tables for Each Factor

Score tables are the elements through which the performance criteria for each incentive factor is established. The score represents the percent of incentive that employees will receive depending on their performance.

A score table consists of three main elements:

- ***threshold*** the minimum level of performance that employees must achieve for each incentive factor before the incentive becomes effective (e.g. 75 percent of goal)
- ***ceiling*** the level at which the incentive will be capped or maximized (let's say at 150 percent of goal)
- ***increment*** the steps at which the incentive will vary, e.g. the incentive compensation can be stepped up every 1%, 2%, 3%, 4%, or 5% of goal achieved.

Generally, it can be assumed that the incentive pay will increase with increased levels of goal attainment.

At the end of the compensation period, the actual result obtained for each incentive factor is compared with its goal and the percent of goal achieved is determined. A corresponding score is assigned to each level of percent of goal achieved.

Table 3.8 on page 31 is an example of a score table. This table shows the score an employee will receive if they reach between 75 percent and 125 percent of the goal for a specific incentive factor. Per this example, a person is entitled to a score of 100 points if they reach 90 percent of the goal. The score is higher as higher percentages of the goal are reached. Below 75 percent the score is zero. In this particular example, the measurements are made in 5 percent increments; however, score tables are totally flexible and can be set according to each company's needs.

Table 3.8 Score Table for Sales Goal Factor

% of Sales Goal Achieved	Score
125%	150
120%	140
115%	130
110%	120
105%	115
100%	110
95%	105
90%	100
85%	90
80%	80
75%	70
Below 75%	0

Threshold = 75%, Ceiling = 125%, Increment = 5%

3.9 *Step Six* – Selecting Compensation Sources

Compensation sources are the financial resources through which the incentive plan is funded. Single or multiple compensation sources can fund the plan. Typically, a certain percent of a compensation source is allocated to fund the plan, e.g. 10 percent of pre-tax profit, 40 percent of budget surplus, 30 percent of increase in profits, etc.

Listed below are some examples of compensation sources:
- Earnings Per Share (EPS)
- EBIT (Earnings Before Interest and Taxes)
- EBITDA (Earnings Before Interest, Taxes, Depreciation and Amortization)
- (EVA) Economic Value Added
- Gross Profit Dollars Earned
- Increase in Profits
- Increase in Sales Dollars
- Net Income
- Pre-Tax Earnings

- Sales Dollars
- Cost Reduction ($)
- Total Revenue ($)
- Return on Investment ($)
- Return on Capital ($)
- Stockholder Return ($)

Table 3.9.1 below shows an example of compensation sources and their allocation to the incentive plan.

Table 3.9.1   Compensation Sources and Percent Allocated to Plan

Compensation Source	Projected Source Revenue	% Allocated	Projected Source Allocation
Pre-Tax Profit	500K	10%	50K
Cost Reduction	50K	50%	25K
Return on Investment	250K	20%	50K
Total Projected Source Allocation			125K

Groups can be linked to the compensation sources they have most control over and influence on, so that there is even more correlation between their performance and their incentive pay. Executives can be allocated a certain percentage of return on investment or return on capital. Finance executives can be allocated a percentage of cost reduction or budget surplus. Sales executives can be allocated a percentage of gross profit dollars earned. Manufacturing employees can be allocated a percentage of cost savings generated from improved productivity, etc.

Using this method, a matrix can be created to allocate the various compensation sources assigned to each group. Table 3.9.2 on *page 33* is an example of the allocation of compensation sources to different groups.

Table 3.9.2   Compensation Sources Allocation to Groups for Company ABC

Incentive Factors	Executive	Engineering	Operations	Sales	Admin.	Total
Pre-Tax Profit		2.0 %	3.0 %	1.0 %	1.0 %	7.0 %
EBIT	3.0 %			1.0 %		4.0 %
Cost Savings			2.0 %		2.0 %	4.0 %
Gross Profit Dollars		1.0 %		3.0 %		4.0 %
Return on Investment	2.0 %				1.0 %	3.0 %
Return on Capital	2.0 %					2.0 %

Earnings Per Share (EPS) can also be used as a universal compensation source for the whole company. It can be used by itself or in combination with other sources. In the Earnings Per Share method, every employee can be allocated a certain number of phantom shares (or if the company prefers, real shares). At the end of the compensation period, the company reports its earnings per share and employees are allocated a compensation source equal to the number of shares they were allocated multiplied by the EPS for that period.

For example, at the end of the first quarter of fiscal year 2000, the company reported earning $ .30/share. The QA supervisor was allocated 3,000 shares by the plan, so the first quarter incentive compensation source from EPS for the supervisor will be: 3,000 x $ .30 = $ 900. If additional compensation sources were allocated to this position, they would be added to the EPS source.

3.10 *Step Seven* – Allocating Compensation Sources

Compensation source allocation is defined as the percentage of the compensation source allocated to each group and then further subdivided to subgroups and individual levels. It is one of the key elements in determining the bonus employees receive at the end of every period. This is your contract with your employees: If they reach the goals, they will be rewarded.

Allocating the compensation source is a sensitive issue that should be addressed with great care. The most suitable approach is to use historical data the company may possess from previous compensation plans, or use related industry compensation benchmarks for variable pay scales.[1] It is critical to allow participants to maintain their earnings levels, but have an incentive to increase earnings with increased levels of performance. Another consideration: the larger the contribution a participant has in generating the corporate income, the larger the compensation source allocation for that particular group or individual.

Group directors and managers should play an active role in determining the compensation source allocation for their group members. These key personnel are responsible for the group performance results; they know their employees well and, therefore, should be an active participant in these decisions.

It is recommended to start with a conservative selection and allocation of compensation sources to the plan. Select one or two sources and allocate a conservative amount that will not be a financial drain, subjecting the company to unnecessary risks. The allocation may be increased once there is a high level of confidence and comfort in the plan. A conservative approach can avoid an initial high allocation, which may result in future cutbacks in compensation allocation. Cutbacks can be a morale blow and should be avoided as much as possible.

Another important point is to reserve some of the incentive plan funding for new employees that may be hired during the year. Typically, 80 percent of the selected compensation source funding should be allocated to the existing workforce while 20 percent remains in reserve.

---

[1] This is published annually by the American Compensation Association (ACA). See www.acaonline.org for further information.

With the allocation of pre-tax profits, for example, even though the company is giving up a "piece of the pie" and decides to give 20 percent of its profits to the employees, the benefits of having a motivated, dedicated, and productive workforce can yield much higher earnings as demonstrated in the hypothetical example below.

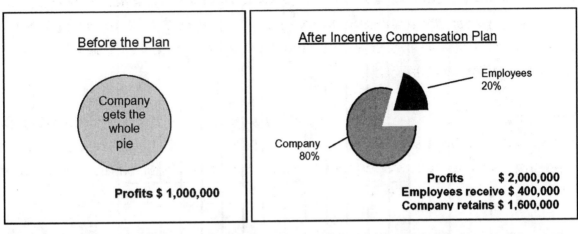

The after-plan scenario shows a $600,000 or 60 percent increase in pre-tax revenue for the company, even though it gave up only 20 percent of its profits.

Table 3.10 on *page 36* demonstrates an example of pre-tax profit dollar allocation for all employees by subgroup. The same process is repeated for any other compensation sources selected for the plan.

3.11 *Step Eight* – Calculating the Bonus

3.11.1 Performance Index

The employees' performance in each incentive factor assigned to them is measured at the end of each compensation period. A score is generated for each factor based on the actual results achieved for that period. The employee score in each factor category is multiplied by the factor weight allocated to it and divided by 100. Adding all factor category scores yields the **performance index** (PI).

Table 3.10   Pre-Tax Profit Allocation per Subgroup

Group	Sub-Group	# of Employees in Sub-Group	% of Profit Allocation per Employee	% of Profit Allocation per Sub-Group	% of Profit Allocation per Group
Executive	CEO	1	1.5	1.5	3.75
	President	1	1.5	1.5	
	QA Manager	1	.75	.75	
Engineering	Director of Engineering	1	.75	.75	1.75
	Configuration Mgmt. Engineer	1	.5	.5	
	Program Engineer	1	.5	.5	
Operations	Operations Manager	1	.75	.75	2.05
	Technical Support Specialist	1	.5	.5	
	Shipping/Receiving Clerk	1	.4	.4	
	Buyer	1	.4	.4	
Sales & Marketing	Director, Sales and Marketing	1	1.2	1.2	4.2
	Sales Executive, Region A	2	.75	1.5	
	Sales Executive, Region B	2	.75	1.5	
Finance/ Admin.	CFO	1	1.5	1.5	3.55
	Administrative Staff	2	.4	.8	
	Accountant	1	.5	.5	
	Comptroller	1	.75	.75	
	Number of Employees: 20				Total Profit Allocation: 15.3 %

The performance index represents the overall employee performance in achieving all the goals assigned to them. The performance index is derived using the following formula:

$$PI = \frac{S1 \times F1}{100} + \frac{S2 \times F2}{100} + \frac{S3 \times F3}{100} + \ldots\ldots \frac{Sn \times Fn}{100}$$

(Performance Index)

Where S1, S2, S3... etc., are scores achieved for each Incentive Factor.
F1, F2, F3... etc., are weights allocated to each factor respectively.
Note that F1+ F2+ F3+...+Fn = 100%

3.11.2 The Compensation Pie (CP)

In sections 3.9 and 3.10 we defined compensation sources and their allocation. What this means is that each person on the plan has a certain slice of the pie allocated to them. In general, most plan participants will have a single compensation source; however, executives may be allocated more than one compensation source.

The value of this pie is determined by adding the values of each compensation source selected for the person multiplied by the percent of that source allocated to them as shown in the formula below:

$$CP = CS_1 \times SA_1 + CS_2 \times SA_2 + CS_3 \times SA_3 + \ldots CS_n \times SA_n$$

(Compensation Pie)

Where CS_1, CS_2, CS_3 ... etc., are the compensation sources.
SA_1, SA_2, SA_3 ... etc., are the percentages allocated to each source respectively.

3.11.3 The Final Bonus

The final bonus is calculated as follows:

$$PB = PI \times CP$$

$$\text{(Periodic Bonus)} \quad \text{(Performance Index)} \quad \text{(Compensation Pie)}$$

Bonus calculations are made periodically, as stated in the compensation schedule. Periodic bonus calculations are normally based on cumulative year-to-date figures. Losses are carried forward to offset profits in subsequent quarters.

Bonus payments are made to eligible employees preferably within 30 days of the last day the compensation period ends.

The company may reserve the right to make adjustments to bonuses paid for the last quarter of each year, should there be considerable changes made to the company's annual profit by the accounting firm auditing the company's financial records. Such adjustments can be made in the first quarter of the following year.

It is important to make the bonus payments in a *timely manner. **Employees expect to be rewarded on time.*** Delay tactics often cause employees to lose faith in the program, which defeats the purpose of implementing the plan in the first place.

3.12 *Step Nine* – Testing the Plan

It is recommended to test the designed plan to **simulate outcomes** based on several forecast models such as low-, intermediate- and high-performance scenarios. This test will assure management that higher performance levels will yield higher profits and higher rewards, that achieving below the minimum performance benchmarks will not be rewarded, and that the company is not at risk of draining financial resources without financial gains.

As a result of the analysis of the plan simulation, **modifications and final adjustments can be made to the plan to verify that it will meet its expectation.** Any changes are re-tested to verify desired outcome.

3.13 *Step Ten* – Approving the Plan

Once all the changes and tests are completed and management is satisfied with all aspects of the plan, the plan design is approved and the implementation stage begins.

CHAPTER FOUR
PERFORMANCE EVALUATION AND PERSONAL OBJECTIVES

4.1 Introduction

Performance evaluation and **personal objectives** may be used as unique incentive factors that have their own set-up and data-entry procedures. The use of either of these factors in an incentive compensation plan is optional. Additionally, these factors can be partially implemented, which means that they can be assigned only to those employees whose job functions are not easily measured by quantitative methods.

Performance evaluation and personal objectives can be used as stand-alone factors or they can be combined with other incentive factors selected for the incentive compensation plan. The importance they play in the compensation scheme is indicated by the weight assigned to them in comparison to other factors. The example in Table 4.1 shows several incentive factors assigned to an employee and their corresponding weights.

Table 4.1 Incentive Factors for Administrative Assistant

Incentive Factors	Weight
Personal Objectives	30%
Performance Evaluation	25%
Total Revenue	25%
Budget Control	20%

These modules can also be used independently of each other or independent of other incentive factors. For example, if an employee's performance is to be measured using only the performance evaluation criteria, then 100 percent weight is assigned to this factor. If two factors are to be used in measuring an employee's performance, then assign 50%-50% weight to each. If they are to be used in conjunction with other incentive factors, Table 4.1 is a good example.

4.2   Performance Evaluation

Performance evaluation is a method to assess the performance of individual employees using predefined **performance categories** established by the company.

4.2.1 Performance Categories

Each performance category should be described explicitly, including a detailed explanation of what is expected of the employee and specific guidelines on how to evaluate the employee's performance.

Performance categories are assigned on an individual basis and need to be clearly understood by all the employees who will be evaluated utilizing this method. Performance categories are required only if the compensation plan is set up to measure personal performance as an incentive factor.

The following list shows examples of performance categories that can be used to establish the criteria for employee performance evaluation:

- Attendance – Measures the punctuality of observing work hours. Managers are expected to monitor and control their department employees and their workload.

- Motivation – Reflects the employee's desire to perform their job to the best of their ability and in the best interests of the corporation.

- Effort – Measures the physical or mental energy put forth by the employee to ensure that duties and assigned tasks are accomplished in a satisfactory and timely manner.

- Efficiency – Measures the effectiveness of performing the daily duties and special assignments, maximizing the utilization of corporate resources.

- Accuracy – Measures the employee's ability to perform their daily duties in an error-free manner, displaying exactitude and thoroughness at each task.

- Assertiveness – Measures the employee's ability to affirm one's opinion in a persuasive, non-confrontational manner with the purpose of facilitating decisions to the benefit of the organization.

- Conflict Management – Measures the employee's ability to prevent conflict in the organizational setting, mediate and negotiate with difficult people and resolve disputes or problems fairly.

- Mentoring – Measures the employee's ability to aid in the development of other employees' potential using constructive feedback and delegation as tools to improve personnel performance while increasing productivity and facilitating organizational change.

- Follow Up — Reflects on the manner in which the employee follows up on:
  (a) Tasks that have to be accomplished on a regular basis
  (b) Instructions and or directions given to them by their superiors
  (c) Instructions and or directions given by them to other employees under their supervision

- Teamwork – Measures the effectiveness of working and coordinating overall efforts with other departments or teams, thus ensuring fast and smooth flow of activities among all departments. The emphasis is on overall corporate effort and working in harmony with others toward reaching the company's goals.

- Meeting Objectives – Measures the ability of the employee to accomplish established objectives and specific tasks assigned by their supervisors in a competent way and within the designated time frame.

- Corrective Action – Measures the responsiveness of the employee to correct problems or actions that have occurred in the past and improve in areas where performance enhancement is required (as pointed out to them in reviews, verbal, and written communications).

4.2.2 Select Performance Categories

For each employee that was assigned the performance evaluation incentive factor, the categories by which they will be evaluated must first be selected. It is recommended to select between four to eight categories for each employee (no more than 10) to allow them to focus their efforts on those categories critical to their job function.

Assigning too many categories can be distracting and confusing and should be avoided.

4.2.3 Allocate Category Weights

A weight is allocated for each performance category selected for an employee based on the importance such a category plays in the employee's performance of their job function. The cumulative weight of all performance categories allocated to each employee must equal 100 percent. Avoid allocating weights of less than 10 percent per factor.

Table 4.2.3 is an example of four performance categories and their allocated weights:

Table 4.2.3   Performance Categories and Allocated Weights

Performance Category	Weight Allocated
Problem-Solving Skills	35%
Effort	25%
Efficiency	25%
Teamwork	15%
Total Weight	**100%**

4.2.4 Performance Rating

A rating system must be established so that managers and supervisors assessing employee performance use a standard scale.

For example, the following performance key may be used:

5 = Excellent
4 = Very good
3 = Acceptable
2 = Marginal
1 = Unacceptable

(0.5 increment may be used for inbetween scores, e.g. 2.5, 3.5, etc.)

4.2.5 Performance Evaluation Score Tables

Score tables define the achievement level expected from the employee. The score represents the percent of the incentive that the employee will receive depending on the rating they achieve. Higher levels of achievement will yield higher scores and consequently increased incentive.

For example, looking at the performance evaluation score table 4.2.5, at a rating of 40, the employee will receive 85 percent of the incentive allocated to this factor. At a rating of 44, the incentive increases to 111 percent and at a score of 50, it increases to 150 percent.

Table 4.2.5   Performance Evaluation Score Table

Weighted-Rating	Score
Min 30	20
32	33
34	46
36	59
38	72
40	85
42	98
44	111
46	124
48	137
Max 50	150

Threshold = 30, Ceiling = 50, Increment = 2.0

NOTE: Maximum rating is 50, minimum rating is 30. A rating below 30 will nullify the portion of the incentive allocated to this factor.

4.2.6 End of Period Review

At the end of each compensation period, the group manager or immediate supervisor meets with the employees to review of their performances. The supervisor will assign a rating to each selected performance category and the employee will have the opportunity to discuss these ratings with the supervisor and provide feedback, comments, and/or suggestions.

Table 4.2.6 is an example of the rating allocated for each of the four performance categories in Table 4.2.3 and their final weighted-rating. The cumulative weighted-rating represents the achievement of the employee in all performance categories.

Table 4.2.6 Rating and Weighted-rating by Categories

Performance Category	Weight Allocated	Rating	Weighted Rating
Problem-solving Skills	35%	3.5	12.25
Effort	25%	5.0	12.5
Efficiency	25%	4.0	10.0
Teamwork	15%	5.0	7.5
Cumulative Weighted-rating			42.25
Score *			98

*The cumulative weighted-rating is converted to a score using the score table created for the performance evaluation factor (see Table 4.2.5). This score, together with the employee's scores in other incentive factors, is used in the final calculation of the incentive compensation bonus.

4.3 Personal Objectives

Personal objectives are specific tasks, projects, jobs, or goals that can be assigned to employees during a compensation period. Typically, the task (or portion of it) should be completed within the compensation period for which it was assigned.

4.3.1 Assigning Objectives

An employee can be assigned several objectives within a compensation period. The supervisor or manager, through consultation with the employee, determines what tasks are to be accomplished during this period.

Several important components must be defined for each assigned objective.

a) **Objective Description**

   The objective must be described in explicit detail so the employee can understand clearly what he or she is expected to accomplish.

b) **Deliverables**

   Deliverables are items such as reports, prototypes, and certification that are to be delivered or obtained by the employee at the completion of the task.

c) **Difficulty Level**

   Every task is assigned a difficulty level on a scale from one to 10 (where one equals easiest and 10 equals hardest). This component measures the relative degree of complexity involved in completing the task. The company may determine that there is a minimum level of difficulty that must be assigned to an employee during a compensation period. For example, if the minimum difficulty level is 18, the supervisor will assign the employee at least two tasks with a difficulty level of nine each or three tasks with a difficulty level of six each.

d) **Priority**

   When more than one task has been assigned, priority defines the sequential order in which the tasks are to be completed. A job with a priority one will be completed first, followed by the job with a priority two, and so on.

e) **Weight**

   Each task is allocated weight. The weight determines the relative importance of the tasks in relation to the other tasks assigned for the same period. The total weight assigned to all the tasks must equal 100 percent.

f) **Due Date**

   Finally, each task is assigned a date by which it should be completed.

Table 4.3.1 is an example of personal assigned objectives.

Table 4.3.1   Personal Objectives Components

Employee Name:			Period:	
Group:				
Objective	Difficulty Level	Priority	Weight	Due Date
Complete internal audits	8	1	40%	1/30/2000
Complete Y2K reports	7	2	30%	2/28/2000
Complete product certification	8	3	30%	3/31/2000
Total	24		100%	

4.3.2   Personal Objectives Score Table

The score table defines the achievement level expected from the employee. Higher levels of completion of personal objectives will yield higher scores and increased incentive. An example of a score table for personal objectives are shown in Table 4.3.2 below.

Table 4.3.2   Personal Objectives Score Table

% of Completion		Score
(Min. expected)	70	30
	75	41
	80	53
	85	65
	90	76
	95	88
(Max.)	100	100

Threshold = 70%, Ceiling = 100%, Increment = 5%

NOTE: Below 70% completion, the value of the incentive allocated to this factor will be nullified.

4.3.3   Difficulty Booster

In order to be fair to employees who are assigned several tasks with a combined difficulty level higher than the minimum required, their scores may be boosted to reflect the added effort put forth to complete these projects.

First, a miniπmbined difficulty level must be determined for all participants using per-sonal objectives, so that everyone gets his fair share of the work. Employees who are assigned higher than the minimum difficulty level will receive boosted scores depending on the total difficulty assigned and how well assignments are completed.

The table below is an example of how scores can be boosted.

Table 4.3.3 Personal Objectives Score Adjustment Table

Total Difficulty Level	Score Adjustment %
20 (Min. Difficulty Level)	100%
22	110%
24	120%
26	130%
28	140%
30	150%
32	160%
34	170%
36	180%
38	190%
40 (Max. Difficulty Level)	200%

Threshold = 20, Ceiling = 40, Increment = 2

For example, an employee completed 100 percent of his tasks, he receives a score of 100 (see Table 4.3.2 on *page 48*). However, if the total difficulty level was 30, the score is now boosted to:

100	x	150%	=	150
(Score)		(Score Adjustment)		(Boosted Score)

4.3.4 End of Period Review

At the end of each compensation period, the group manager or supervisor will meet with the employee and review their final progress on all assigned objectives. Based on this review, a percent of completion will be entered for each objective. Depending on the number of projects and their respective weights, a cumulative percentage of completed objectives will be established for the combined tasks assigned for that period.

Table 4.3.4 is an example of the personal objectives data at the end of the compensation period.

Table 4.3.4   End of Period Review of Personal Objectives

Employee Name:					Period:	
Group:						
Objective	Difficulty Level	Priority	Due Date	Weight	% Completion	Weighted Completion
Complete internal audits	8	1	1/30	40%	100	40%
Complete Y2K reports	7	2	2/28	30%	100	30%
Complete product certification	8	3	3/31	30%	90	27%
Totals	24			100%		97%
					Score	88
					Adjusted Score	106

The score for 97 percent completion is 88 points (see Table 4.3.2 on page 48). The score adjustment, due to the higher difficulty level of 24 is 120 percent (see Table 4.3.3 on page 49), so the final score is, 88 x 120% = 106 points (rounded). This score, together with the employee's scores in other incentive factors, is used in the final calculation of the incentive compensation bonus.

CHAPTER FIVE
PLAN IMPLEMENTATION, ADMINISTRATION, AND MONITORING

5.1 Plan Implementation

Once the plan design stage is finalized, attention is turned to the plan implementation process. Figure 5.1 shows a flowchart of the five steps in the plan implementation.

Fig. 5.1 Plan Implementation Flowchart

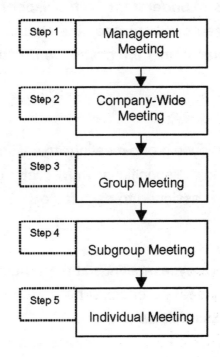

Step 1 — Management Meeting
Step 2 — Company-Wide Meeting
Step 3 — Group Meeting
Step 4 — Subgroup Meeting
Step 5 — Individual Meeting

5.1.1 Management Meeting

The first step in the implementation phase of an incentive plan is to call for a corporate management meeting for all levels of management to explain the plan thoroughly, gather input and feedback and set up an implementation schedule for the plan.

Management personnel will be responsible for the plan execution and administration within the workforce ranks. Their enthusiastic participation and cooperation is critical to the overall success of the plan. The company should put together an "Implementation Team" that will be directly responsible for the successful execution of the incentive plan and report its progress to top management. The team should incorporate representatives from the various functional groups such as HR, Finance, IT, Engineering, Manufacturing, QA, Business Development, etc.

5.1.2 Company-Wide Meetings
The second step is to hold a meeting with all employees to review the plan, explain the details, and answer any questions and/or concerns that employees may have. It is important for *all employees to understand all the aspects of the plan* and how their performance and achievements will influence the company's success and their personal gains. *An ambiguous plan can cause confusion and yield unfavorable results*.

5.1.3 Group Meetings
The third step is to hold employee group meetings to ensure that all employees in each group review and understand the specific incentive factor goals that they will be measured against and the weight assigned to each factor.

5.1.4 Subgroup Meetings
The fourth step is to hold employee meetings at the subgroup or functional-team level to ensure that all employees in each subgroup review and understand the specific details of the plan as it relates to them.

5.1.5 Individual Meetings
The group administrator will meet with each individual in the group to review the following in a confidential manner:
a) The compensation sources assigned to them.
b) The percent of the compensation sources allocated to them.
c) Any questions or concerns they have regarding the plan.

For a successful implementation of the incentive plan, it is imperative that employees clearly understand how they are expected to perform. The most practical way to accomplish this is by demonstrating the incentive compensation calculation method through various hypothetical examples, showing how different outcomes influence compensation payments. Each employee will be presented with a report detailing their goals, weight allocation, compensation pie and their projected incentive pay if they achieve 100 percent of the goals. This is the *"carrot"* that will persuade them to think, "If I accomplish this; I will get that!" Simultaneously, this report will convey to the employees the message of earnest commitment to the plan from the company's executives.

The result: employees will maximize their performance in order to maximize their rewards. Again, the emphasis is on *clarity and understanding* of the plan. Without it, employees may not realize what they are expected to accomplish in order to maximize performance and rewards.

5.2 Plan Administration

When all employees are clear on what is expected of them and how their performances influence their rewards, an administrative system should be put in place to gather data, enter periodic performance, calculate the compensation payout, and manage the compensation payout process.

These tasks and calculations can be performed automatically by the IncentPower™ software program, which will greatly speed and simplify the compensation plan administration and payout process. This innovative tool can be ordered from IncenSoft LLC., additional information on IncenSoft™ and IncentPower™ are available by logging onto www.incensoft.com or calling 1-888-393-3255.

IncentPower™ will allow you to perform the following functions in the process of putting your incentive plan in action:

(i) **Setup Functions for All the Aspects of your Plan**
- Create groups and subgroups
- Create incentive factors

- Assign incentive factors to groups
- Allocate incentive factors to subgroups
- Assign weights to factors at the subgroup level
- Set quantitative goals for each incentive factor
- Setup a compensation schedule for each group
- Setup performance score tables for each incentive factor
- Select compensation sources
- Allocate compensation sources to groups and subgroups
- Enter all plan participants into the program
- Setup a performance evaluation criteria for each employee
- Assign personal objectives (projects) to each employee

(ii) End of Period Data Entry and Processing Functions
- Enter actual performance data for each incentive factor
- Enter actual compensation source data
- On-line manager/employee performance and personal objectives review
- Calculate incentive compensation automatically

(iii) Administrative Functions
- Database Management
- Security Setup (four levels)
- Archive
- Bonus Approval
- Payment Authorization
- Year-end Closing

(iv) Reporting Functions
- Setup Reports (5)
    - Groups/Factors Allocation
    - Factors/Score Table by Group
    - Compensation Source Allocation by Group
    - Group Compensation Allocation
    - Factor Weights Allocation by Group

- Employee Bonus Reports (4)
    - Projected Bonus Calculation
    - Employee Bonus Calculation
    - Bonus Authorization and History
    - Combined Employee Report
- Employee Performance Reports (2)
    - Performance Evaluation by Employee
    - Employee Personal Objectives Report
- Group Summary Reports (2)
    - Group Bonus Summary
    - Factor Goals vs. Actual Performance by Group
- Company Bonus Reports (5)
    - Company-wide Bonus
    - Compensation Allocation and Payout
    - Financial Summary (monthly)
    - Financial Summary (bi-weekly)
    - Long-term Goals

The functions performed by the software represent substantial time and costs savings to companies engaged in the implementation, administration and maintenance of incentive compensation plans. It will ease the administrative time-consuming burden from managers, HR personnel, finance personnel, and executives. Successful implementation of IncentPower™ will allow businesses to enhance their productivity, increase employee loyalty and retention, boost morale, and improve earnings.

In the absence of the IncentPower™ software, a manual or semi-manual system has to be put in place to administer all the functions described in this book.

5.3 Plan Monitoring and Feedback
The program progress and success will be monitored through three main mechanisms:

5.3.1 Supervisor and Employee Feedback from Periodic Reviews
The supervisors' open discussion with employees during the review process will

facilitate the employees' feedback. To this feedback, supervisors add their own assessment of the plan progress. A summary of these reports will be submitted for management's review or they can be presented at a management review meeting.

5.3.2 Management's Review of Plan Success through:
a) Measuring the progress of attaining company goals.
b) Getting personally involved with discussing the plan, its effectiveness and success with various employee groups at all levels.
c) Making sure employees are rewarded fairly and equitably for their efforts and performance.
d) Monitoring employee's performance improvement efforts.

5.3.3 Employee Surveys
Employee job assessment surveys provide management with quick feedback regarding the success of the plan. If survey scores are higher than the initial program survey and job satisfaction is on the rise, the program is progressing well. If scores are lower than the initial program survey, the program is not on the right track.

Employee Surveys should be conducted at least once a year, however, it is strongly recommended to conduct a second survey within six to nine months of the incentive program "kick off" to provide management with an early indication of the program's progress.

All comments, suggestions, and objections gathered by the above three mechanisms are reviewed and discussed by management and, when necessary, changes are instituted to ensure the plan is a success.

5.3.4 Goals Review Meeting
Approximately 15–20 days after the end of every quarter, a management goal review and progress meeting will be held with *all employees in attendance*. Company management will review the past quarter results and compare them with the goals for the same period. An analysis of the company's financial results is provided to all employ-

ees. In addition, the company's future prospects and long-term goals are reviewed and restated. Table 5.3 below is an example of a quarterly management review form.

Table 5.3   Periodic Management Review

Period Ending: December 31st		Year : 2000	
Factors	Goals	Actual	% Achieved
Sales	10,000,000	11,000,000	110%
Profit Before Taxes	750,000	850,000	113%
Stockholder Equity	1,000,000	1,050,000	105%
Gross Profit Margin (GPM)	36%	38%	105%
New Product Development	2	3	150%
Increase Market Share	16%	18%	112%
Increase Customer Satisfaction	95%	97%	102%
Share Value of Stock	$ 6.00	$ 7.00	116%

The company needs to share important information with its employees and encourage everyone to **get involved, provide feedback,** and **contribute to the company's stability and success. Uninformed employees cannot react to unknown conditions!** It is critical to conduct the management quarterly reviews on time and keep employees informed and involved in the company's plan and its progress.

It is recommended to combine such meetings with a social event such as a company luncheon, service award presentation, birthday party, etc. This will help boost morale and maximize attendance.

CHAPTER SIX
THE SURVEY PROCESS

6.1 Introduction

Employee surveys are critical in assessing the company's performance as viewed by its workforce. Employees can provide insightful feedback to management as to what areas within the organization are lacking attention and what is important to the company's success from the employees' point of view.

It is strongly recommended to conduct a survey at the start-up stage of the incentive compensation program to determine the motivational and demotivational issues affecting the workforce and to get valuable information required for the design of the plan. The first survey will also create a base line **survey index** for comparative purposes in future surveys. In other words, future surveys should show improvement in the survey index versus the initial results.

Employee surveys should be conducted *at least once a year*; however, it is strongly recommended to conduct a second survey within six to nine months of the incentive program "kick off," to provide management with an early indication of the program's progress.

A complete survey example with questionnaire, tabulated results, and graphic output is provided in Section 6.8 of this chapter.

Refer to Chapter 2, Section 2.5, Surveying Employees, *for additional information on the purpose and method of surveying employees.*

6.2 Designing the Survey Format

- The survey format is designed to match the company's specific needs, environment and nature of business. Choose questions from the survey example in Section 6.8. Add or delete questions to fit your company requirements. Refer to *page 65* for a list of additional survey questions you may select from.

- The rating system employees use to voice their opinion should be simple, clear, and easy to understand.

- The survey form should include a blank section at the bottom where employees can include their comments and/or suggestions.

- The rating system has to be balanced so as not to stress positive or negative. An example of such a rating system is shown below and used in the survey.

Completely Satisfied	= 5 (Best Rating)
Highly Satisfied	= 4
Moderately Satisfied	= 3
Somewhat Dissatisfied	= 2
Not Satisfied	= 1 (Worst Rating)

6.3 Conducting the Survey

The Human Resources department of the company can conduct the survey. Alternatively, an outside firm specializing in surveys and polls can be outsourced to provide this service in a strictly confidential manner.

Surveys need to be conducted in a confidential, neutral, and pressure-free atmosphere so employees can voice their opinions freely.

Two or three days should be scheduled in which to take the survey, maximizing responses and minimizing absenteism.

The survey should be conducted in a private room, group by group. Survey forms or computerized survey screens should not indicate names or any employee identifying code, instead they should be marked with the group code and a sequential number. There should be no link between the employees taking the survey and their responses.

The survey questions and the rating system should be explained thoroughly to every group before starting. Each group will be given sufficient time to answer the survey and provided assistance as necessary. Once completed, the surveyor gives each employee a gift designated by the company. (This item is optional but recommended.)

Survey forms are left for absent employees with a self-addressed, stamped envelope to be completed and mailed within a limited period of time (one to two weeks preferably). If an electronic survey tool is used, the whole process can be conducted on the company's intranet or on the Internet.

An example of an Employee Survey Memo and Questionnaire are provided on pages 67-69.

6.4 Compiling the Results

When all the survey results are in, they are sorted by group and counted. Each group should have a minimum of two thirds (67 percent) of the surveys returned for the data to be significant.

The higher the participation rates, the more accurate and meaningful the results. The goal is to reach participation levels of 80 percent and higher. This indicates employee interest in voicing their opinion and confidence that their opinion will make a difference.

Each group data is tabulated in a spreadsheet by survey categories and questions. See survey example by group, *pages 70-85.* An average for each survey question and category, and an overall group average are calculated automatically by the spreadsheet for each group. Category averages are plotted by group to provide a graphic display of the results, see *pages 82-84*.

When all group data is complete, the average results for each group are tabulated by line items in a spreadsheet representing results for the entire company. For each survey line item, an overall company average is calculated automatically as shown in the last column on *pages 80 and 81*.

The overall company average for each category and for each group is plotted to provide a graphic display of the survey results, see *page 85*. An ***overall company survey score,*** which is the average of all survey categories for the entire company, is generated from the spreadsheet automatically, see *page 81*. ***The term "survey index" is used to describe this average***. This is an indicator of what employees think of the company and areas of content and discontent. Management's objective is to continuously improve and maximize the survey index and make sure areas of discontent are ***addressed and resolved***.

6.5 Analysis of Survey Results

Survey results should first examine responses on a group level. Each group may have different needs and may be subjected to different environmental and work conditions. For example, office employees operate in a different environment than manufacturing employees or outside sales people.

Therefore, each group's survey should be analyzed in reference to its unique characteristics and environment. This way the company can address each group's specific needs. Employee comments and suggestions should be examined to determine areas of concern or identify areas of strength. Look for a repeating pattern rather than isolated opinions. For example, if 30 percent of employees suggest additional training, this is a valid point. On the other hand if only one group member out of 20 complains bitterly about working conditions, this is probably an isolated case.

After each group is examined individually, attention is turned to the combined results for the whole company. Try to find a correlation between the responses of the various groups to the same line items and their comments. Again try to find parallel patterns to help isolate problems and then deal with them effectively.

Any survey line item with an overall company average of 2.5 and less should be examined carefully to identify the source of the problem and devise a remedy.

6.6 Survey Conclusions and Recommendations

This section delineates the major conclusions of the survey and recommends a course of action to address and resolve the main areas of concern identified by the survey.

6.6.1 Survey Conclusions

Survey conclusions are classified into the following three categories:

U = Urgent Need for Improvement

This category describes an area of extreme major concern to employees, which is a high priority for resolution (within one to two months).

S = Strong Need for Improvement

Here employees have a major concern that needs to be addressed, however the resolution is of a secondary priority (within two to three months).

A = Area of Concern

This category identifies areas in which employees voiced concern. Such areas should be monitored closely over the next six months. They may be resolved with time or may escalate to a point where a resolution will become essential.

Each group response should be reviewed in order to identify *problem areas*. The scores and the employee comments determine problem areas. Survey conclusions are tabulated by identifiable problem areas and groups.

The example in Table 6.6.1 shows the findings of a survey conducted among five groups, where:

U = Urgent need for improvement

S = Strong need for improvement

A = Area of concern

Table 6.6.1 Problem Areas per Group

Problem Areas List	Group A	Group B	Group C	Group D	Group E
1. Work setting environment	S				S
2. Linkage of job performance to reward	S			U	
3. Limited promotion and growth potential				U	A
4. Income level	S			U	
5. Develop backup plans for critical positions		S			
6. Improve communication	S	S		A	
7. Cooperation between people and departments	S				U
8. Need for training		S		S	U

Survey line items within the group with averages below 2.0 are considered as "U" = Urgent Need for Improvement. An average between 2.0 to 2.5 is considered as "S" = Strong Need for improvement. An average between 2.5 to 3.0 is classified as "A" = Area of Concern. In addition, any areas in the employee comments that show repeated and consistent concern should be added to the problem area list and classified in one of the above categories.

When the table is complete look for problem areas that are identified by more than one group. Such areas show further escalation of the problem since more than one group is voicing concern. Assign a **high priority** to these problem areas.

6.6.2 Recommendations

Through the analysis of the problem areas indicated in the survey, the sources of such problems are identified. Once the source of each problem is identified, a solution is proposed to remedy the condition. In some cases further investigation and research may be required to find the proper answer. This may include interviewing employees to shed more light on the problem, extract an insider view of the conditions that caused discontent, and uncover possible solutions.

Finally, the survey results, conclusions and recommendations are made available to all employees, including management's response and action plan to implement the improvements. *Informed employees will see that management is acting on its promises and will be more helpful, receptive, and cooperative in promoting solutions.*

Table 6.6.2 on *page 66* can be used to outline a plan to implement the survey recommendations.

6.7 Additional Selections for Survey Questionnaire

1. Do you have a sense of job security?
2. Do you receive appreciation from supervisors and management for a job well done?
3. Do you feel that there is teamwork and cooperation within the company?
4. Are all employees working in harmony to reach a common goal?
5. Do you have a sense of pride in the job and feel part of the company?
6. Do you believe in the long-term success of the company?
7. Do you feel that there is a good future here?
8. Does the company communicate its goals and performance to employees?
9. Does the company provide you with the right tools and support to perform your job effectively?
10. Does the company uphold product quality and customer satisfaction?
11. Do you receive sufficient training, instructions, and skill development to perform tasks efficiently?
12. Are you confident that management is doing a good job in creating a successful company with a bright future?
13. Are you confident that management does its best to protect the interest of employees?
14. Is management fair and supportive toward employees?

15. Does management recognize and appreciate employee efforts and performance?

16. Does management provide sufficient motivation and incentive programs for all employees?

Table 6.6.2   Survey Recommendations Implementation Plan

Problem Areas Identified	Urgency Level	Proposed Solution	Budget	Time Table
1. Need for training	U	Identify training needs and perform company-wide training as per schedule	$ 20,000	3/30/00
2. Linkage of job performance to reward	U	Revise and update incentive compensation plan to include all departments in the company	$ 5,000	3/30/00
3. Income level	U	Revise and revamp salary compensation program	$ 5,000	3/30/00
4. Cooperation between people and departments	U	Perform teamwork and conflict resolution in-house seminar	$ 2,000	3/30/00
5. Limited promotion and growth potential	U	Develop internal professional development program	$ 5,000	4/30/00
6. Improve communication	S	Implement Intranet and E-mail access for all office employees	$ 10,000	4/30/00
7. Work setting environment	S	Develop and conduct facilities maintenance plan	$ 5,000	5/30/00
8. Develop backup plans for critical positions	S	Identify critical position and generate backup procedures and training for backup personnel	$ 5,000	6/30/00

The recommendations are listed and addressed in the order of priority ("U", "S", "A"). They provide management with clear-cut, detailed directions on how problem areas should be addressed and resolved. Cost estimates and time schedules should be included as necessary to expedite this process.

6.8   Employee Survey Example

This section incorporates a sample of a survey introduction memo to employees, an employee survey form and the tabulated and graphic results of the sample survey. This memo and survey form can be modified as needed and used to conduct a survey in your organization.

MEMORANDUM

DATE: April 25, 2000
TO: ALL ASSOCIATES
FROM: HUMAN RESOURCES
RE: EMPLOYEE SURVEY

We are pleased to announce that our annual employee survey will take place on April 25-26, 2000. This survey is intended to give management a realistic idea of employee satisfaction levels pertaining to specific job functions, work environment, and other issues. It will provide management insight into the areas in which the company needs to improve the level of support to employees so productivity and earnings continue to rise.

Please be assured that management gives this survey serious consideration, and completed surveys are kept strictly confidential. Management recognizes the significance of employee input, and it is our goal to incorporate employees' input about their jobs and the company into positive results to benefit employees and the company.

Please fill out the survey by circling the number corresponding to the level of satisfaction you feel about the subject matter. Upon completion, place your survey form into the area designated by the surveyor.

The following rating system is used in this survey.

Completely Satisfied	= 5 (Best Rating)
Highly Satisfied	= 4
Moderately Satisfied	= 3
Somewhat Dissatisfied	= 2
Not Satisfied	= 1 (Worst Rating)

CONFIDENTIAL EMPLOYEE SURVEY		GROUP				Date		
No. in Group	**No. Participating in Survey**		**% of Participation**					Average
RATING FACTOR			5	4	3	2	1	
CATEGORY A: PAY & BENEFITS								
How does your Income (salary) compare to similar jobs within the local area?								
How do the company Benefits (Health, Dental, Disability, Life, Vacation, Holidays, etc.) compare to similar companies within the local area?								
How do the Retirement Benefits (401K matching and profit sharing) compare to similar companies within the local area?								
SUBTOTAL								
CATEGORY B: JOB SATISFACTION								
Do you feel a sense of achievement and job accomplishment?								
Do you feel you have the ability to provide input and influence decisions related to job performance?								
Do you feel that your job is secure?								
Are you able to take initiative and make improvements in job performance and work environment issues in the company?								
SUBTOTAL								
CATEGORY C: RECOGNITION AND PROMOTION								
Do you feel recognized and treated fairly by supervisors and the Company in general?								
Do you feel that there is potential for internal promotions and career growth within the Company?								
Do you feel that job performance and personal output is linked to reward (income, bonus and profit sharing)?								
Do you feel appreciated by your supervisor/ management for a job well done?								
SUBTOTAL								
CATEGORY D: CORPORATE ENVIRONMENT								
Do you feel employees display teamwork and cooperation to reach a common goal?								
Do you feel there is a friendly and upbeat atmosphere at work and high moral among all employees?								

CONFIDENTIAL EMPLOYEE SURVEY	GROUP						Date	

No. in Group		No. Participating in Survey		% of Participation					Average
			RATING FACTOR	5	4	3	2	1	
CATEGORY D: CORPORATE ENVIRONMENT (continuation)									
Are you happy and proud of being part of the Company and believe in its successful future?									
Do you feel the Company has enough social activities, such as luncheons, parties and picnics, to make it a pleasant work environment?									
Is your work area clean & comfortable, well lit, and overall do you feel that the Company has a nice facility?									
			SUBTOTAL						
CATEGORY E: COMPANY'S PERFORMANCE									
Are the Company's rules and procedures appropriate and fair?									
Does the Company communicate goals and performance results to all employees?									
Have you been provide with correct tools and support to perform your job effectively?									
Do you feel there is emphasis on product quality and customer focus?									
Have you received sufficient training, instructions and skill development to perform tasks efficiently?									
			SUBTOTAL						
CATEGORY F: MANAGEMENT PERFORMANCE									
Are you confident that Management is doing a good job in creating a successful Company with a bright future?									
Are you confidence that Management will do its best to protect the interest of the employees?									
Is Management fair and supportive towards employees?									
Does Management recognize and appreciate employees' efforts and performance?									
Does Management provide sufficient motivation and incentive programs for employees?									
			SUBTOTAL						
			TOTALS						

<u>Comments / Suggestions:</u> (enter in space below)

| No. in Group: | 29 | No. Participating in Survey | 25 | % of Participation | 86% | |

RATING FACTOR	5	4	3	2	1	Average
CATEGORY A: PAY & BENEFITS						
How does your Income (salary) compare to similar jobs within the local area?	1	1	10	5	8	2.28
How do the company Benefits (Health, Dental, Disability, Life, Vacation, Holidays, etc.) compare to similar companies within the local area?	0	5	8	11	1	2.68
How do the Retirement Benefits (401K matching and profit sharing) compare to similar companies within the local area?	0	9	8	8	0	3.04
SUBTOTAL	1	15	26	24	9	2.67
CATEGORY B: JOB SATISFACTION						
Do you feel a sense of achievement and job accomplishment?	1	6	13	3	2	3.04
Do you feel you have the ability to provide input and influence decisions related to job performance?	0	7	10	6	2	2.88
Do you feel that your job is secure?	4	5	12	3	1	3.32
Are you able to take initiative and make improvements in job performance and work environment issues in the company?	1	8	10	3	3	3.04
SUBTOTAL	6	26	45	15	8	3.07
CATEGORY C: RECOGNITION AND PROMOTION						
Do you feel recognized and treated fairly by supervisors and the Company in general?	1	6	9	3	6	2.72
Do you feel that there is potential for internal promotions and career growth within the Company?	1	4	12	3	5	2.72
Do you feel that job performance and personal output is linked to reward (income, bonus and profit sharing)?	2	3	11	6	3	2.80
Do you feel appreciated by your supervisor/ management for a job well done?	2	5	7	5	6	2.68
SUBTOTAL	6	18	39	17	20	2.73
CATEGORY D: CORPORATE ENVIRONMENT						
Do you feel employees display teamwork and cooperation to reach a common goal?	3	5	12	2	3	3.12
Do you feel there is a friendly and upbeat atmosphere at work and high moral among all employees?	1	7	12	3	2	3.08

CONFIDENTIAL EMPLOYEE SURVEY COMPANY ABC		GROUP A – MANUFACTURING					April 25, 2000	
No. in Group:	**29**	**No. Participating in Survey**	**25**	**% of Participation**		**86%**		Average
RATING FACTOR			**5**	**4**	**3**	**2**	**1**	
CATEGORY D: CORPORATE ENVIRONMENT (continuation)								
Are you happy and proud of being part of the Company and believe in its successful future?			4	7	10	1	3	3.32
Do you feel the Company has enough social activities, such as luncheons, parties and picnics, to make it a pleasant work environment?			10	13	2	0	0	4.32
Is your work area clean & comfortable, well lit, and overall do you feel that the Company has a nice facility?			4	10	6	1	3	3.46
SUBTOTAL			22	42	42	7	11	3.46
CATEGORY E: COMPANY'S PERFORMANCE								
Are the Company's rules and procedures appropriate and fair?			4	8	8	3	2	3.36
Does the Company communicate goals and performance results to all employees?			4	8	5	4	2	3.35
Have you been provide with correct tools and support to perform your job effectively?			1	9	9	4	2	3.12
Do you feel there is emphasis on product quality and customer focus?			3	7	11	2	2	3.28
Have you received sufficient training, instructions and skill development to perform tasks efficiently?			1	7	10	4	3	2.96
SUBTOTAL			13	39	43	17	11	3.21
CATEGORY F: MANAGEMENT PERFORMANCE								
Are you confident that Management is doing a good job in creating a successful Company with a bright future?			3	5	12	2	3	3.12
Are you confidence that Management will do its best to protect the interest of the employees?			6	4	9	4	2	3.32
Is Management fair and supportive towards employees?			1	8	8	4	4	2.92
Does Management recognize and appreciate employees' efforts and performance?			2	4	7	10	2	2.76
Does Management provide sufficient motivation and incentive programs for employees?			1	5	9	6	4	2.72
SUBTOTAL			13	26	45	26	15	2.97
TOTALS			61	166	240	106	74	3.018

<u>Comments / Suggestions:</u> (enter in space below)

CONFIDENTIAL EMPLOYEE SURVEY COMPANY ABC		GROUP B – ADMINISTRATION			April 25, 2000				
No. in Group	10	No. Participating in Survey	9	% of Participation			90%		Average
			RATING FACTOR	5	4	3	2	1	
CATEGORY A: PAY & BENEFITS									
How does your Income (salary) compare to similar jobs within the local area?				0	1	4	3	1	2.56
How do the company Benefits (Health, Dental, Disability, Life, Vacation, Holidays, etc.) compare to similar companies within the local area?				2	3	3	0	1	3.56
How do the Retirement Benefits (401K matching and profit sharing) compare to similar companies within the local area?				3	6	0	0	0	4.33
			SUBTOTAL	5	10	7	3	2	3.48
CATEGORY B: JOB SATISFACTION									
Do you feel a sense of achievement and job accomplishment?				0	2	4	3	0	2.89
Do you feel you have the ability to provide input and influence decisions related to job performance?				0	1	5	2	1	2.67
Do you feel that your job is secure?				2	4	3	0	0	3.89
Are you able to take initiative and make improvements in job performance and work environment issues in the company?				0	3	4	1	1	3.00
			SUBTOTAL	2	10	16	6	2	3.11
CATEGORY C: RECOGNITION AND PROMOTION									
Do you feel recognized and treated fairly by supervisors and the Company in general?				2	3	1	1	2	3.22
Do you feel that there is potential for internal promotions and career growth within the Company?				0	1	5	1	2	2.56
Do you feel that job performance and personal output is linked to reward (income, bonus and profit sharing)?				0	3	2	2	2	2.67
Do you feel appreciated by your supervisor/ management for a job well done?				2	3	1	0	3	3.11
			SUBTOTAL	4	10	9	4	9	2.89
CATEGORY D: CORPORATE ENVIRONMENT									
Do you feel employees display teamwork and cooperation to reach a common goal?				0	3	3	2	1	2.89
Do you feel there is a friendly and upbeat atmosphere at work and high moral among all employees?				1	4	2	0	2	3.22

CONFIDENTIAL EMPLOYEE SURVEY COMPANY ABC	GROUP B – ADMINISTRATION					April 25, 2000	

No. in Group	10	No. Participating in Survey	9	% of Participation		90%	Average
		RATING FACTOR	5	4	3	2	1	

CATEGORY D: CORPORATE ENVIRONMENT (continuation)	5	4	3	2	1	Average
Are you happy and proud of being part of the Company and believe in its successful future?	1	5	0	1	2	3.22
Do you feel the Company has enough social activities, such as luncheons, parties and picnics, to make it a pleasant work environment?	6	1	2	0	0	4.44
Is your work area clean & comfortable, well lit, and overall do you feel that the Company has a nice facility?	4	4	1	0	0	4.33
SUBTOTAL	12	17	8	3	5	3.62

CATEGORY E: COMPANY'S PERFORMANCE	5	4	3	2	1	Average
Are the Company's rules and procedures appropriate and fair?	1	4	2	1	1	3.33
Does the Company communicate goals and performance results to all employees?	1	6	2	0	0	3.89
Have you been provide with correct tools and support to perform your job effectively?	2	5	0	2	0	3.78
Do you feel there is emphasis on product quality and customer focus?	1	3	4	1	0	3.44
Have you received sufficient training, instructions and skill development to perform tasks efficiently?	1	1	3	4	0	9
SUBTOTAL	6	19	11	8	1	3.47

CATEGORY F: MANAGEMENT PERFORMANCE	5	4	3	2	1	Average
Are you confident that Management is doing a good job in creating a successful Company with a bright future?	1	3	2	2	1	3.11
Are you confidence that Management will do its best to protect the interest of the employees?	1	2	3	3	0	3.11
Is Management fair and supportive towards employees?	1	3	2	3	0	3.22
Does Management recognize and appreciate employees' efforts and performance?	0	3	3	2	1	2.89
Does Management provide sufficient motivation and incentive programs for employees?	1	3	1	3	1	3.00
SUBTOTAL	4	14	11	13	3	3.07
TOTALS	33	80	62	37	22	3.273

<u>Comments / Suggestions:</u> (enter in space below)

CONFIDENTIAL EMPLOYEE SURVEY COMPANY ABC	GROUP C - SALES					April 25, 2000	

No. in Group	7	No. Participating in Survey	7	% of Participation		100%	

RATING FACTOR	5	4	3	2	1	Average
CATEGORY A: PAY & BENEFITS						
How does your Income (salary) compare to similar jobs within the local area?	1	0	4	2	0	3.00
How do the company Benefits (Health, Dental, Disability, Life, Vacation, Holidays, etc.) compare to similar companies within the local area?	0	2	3	2	0	3.00
How do the Retirement Benefits (401K matching and profit sharing) compare to similar companies within the local area?	2	2	3	0	0	3.86
SUBTOTAL	3	4	10	4	0	3.29
CATEGORY B: JOB SATISFACTION						
Do you feel a sense of achievement and job accomplishment?	0	2	5	0	0	3.29
Do you feel you have the ability to provide input and influence decisions related to job performance?	0	2	2	1	2	2.57
Do you feel that your job is secure?	2	0	3	2	0	3.29
Are you able to take initiative and make improvements in job performance and work environment issues in the company?	1	1	2	2	1	2.86
SUBTOTAL	3	5	12	5	3	3.00
CATEGORY C: RECOGNITION AND PROMOTION						
Do you feel recognized and treated fairly by supervisors and the Company in general?	2	0	3	2	0	3.29
Do you feel that there is potential for internal promotions and career growth within the Company?	1	0	4	1	1	2.86
Do you feel that job performance and personal output is linked to reward (income, bonus and profit sharing)?	0	1	5	0	1	2.86
Do you feel appreciated by your supervisor/ management for a job well done?	1	0	5	0	1	3.00
SUBTOTAL	4	1	17	3	3	3.00
CATEGORY D: CORPORATE ENVIRONMENT						
Do you feel employees display teamwork and cooperation to reach a common goal?	0	0	3	3	1	2.29
Do you feel there is a friendly and upbeat atmosphere at work and high moral among all employees?	1	1	4	0	1	3.14

No. in Group	7	No. Participating in Survey	7	% of Participation		100%	

RATING FACTOR	5	4	3	2	1	Average
CATEGORY D: CORPORATE ENVIRONMENT (continuation)						
Are you happy and proud of being part of the Company and believe in its successful future?	1	2	2	1	1	3.14
Do you feel the Company has enough social activities, such as luncheons, parties and picnics, to make it a pleasant work environment?	1	2	4	0	0	3.57
Is your work area clean & comfortable, well lit, and overall do you feel that the Company has a nice facility?	1	2	2	1	1	3.14
SUBTOTAL	4	7	15	5	4	3.06
CATEGORY E: COMPANY'S PERFORMANCE						
Are the Company's rules and procedures appropriate and fair?	1	1	3	1	1	3.00
Does the Company communicate goals and performance results to all employees?	1	1	2	3	0	3.00
Have you been provide with correct tools and support to perform your job effectively?	0	1	5	0	1	2.86
Do you feel there is emphasis on product quality and customer focus?	0	2	3	2	0	3.00
Have you received sufficient training, instructions and skill development to perform tasks efficiently?	0	1	5	1	0	3.00
SUBTOTAL	2	6	18	7	2	2.97
CATEGORY F: MANAGEMENT PERFORMANCE						
Are you confident that Management is doing a good job in creating a successful Company with a bright future?	1	1	4	0	1	3.14
Are you confidence that Management will do its best to protect the interest of the employees?	1	2	3	0	1	3.29
Is Management fair and supportive towards employees?	2	0	4	0	1	3.29
Does Management recognize and appreciate employees' efforts and performance?	1	1	4	0	1	3.14
Does Management provide sufficient motivation and incentive programs for employees?	0	1	5	0	1	2.86
SUBTOTAL	5	5	20	0	5	3.14
TOTALS	21	28	92	24	17	3.076

Comments / Suggestions: (enter in space below)

CONFIDENTIAL EMPLOYEE SURVEY COMPANY ABC	GROUP D - ENGINEERING					April 25, 2000	

No. in Group	10	No. Participating in Survey	8	% of Participation		80%	Average

RATING FACTOR	5	4	3	2	1	Average
CATEGORY A: PAY & BENEFITS						
How does your Income (salary) compare to similar jobs within the local area?	0	1	2	3	2	2.25
How do the company Benefits (Health, Dental, Disability, Life, Vacation, Holidays, etc.) compare to similar companies within the local area?	1	3	2	2	0	3.38
How do the Retirement Benefits (401K matching and profit sharing) compare to similar companies within the local area?	1	3	3	0	1	3.38
SUBTOTAL	2	7	7	5	3	3.00
CATEGORY B: JOB SATISFACTION						
Do you feel a sense of achievement and job accomplishment?	2	3	3	0	0	3.88
Do you feel you have the ability to provide input and influence decisions related to job performance?	0	4	3	1	0	3.38
Do you feel that your job is secure?	0	4	4	0	0	3.50
Are you able to take initiative and make improvements in job performance and work environment issues in the company?	1	6	1	0	0	4.00
SUBTOTAL	3	17	11	1	0	3.69
CATEGORY C: RECOGNITION AND PROMOTION						
Do you feel recognized and treated fairly by supervisors and the Company in general?	0	4	3	1	0	3.38
Do you feel that there is potential for internal promotions and career growth within the Company?	0	2	4	0	2	2.75
Do you feel that job performance and personal output is linked to reward (income, bonus and profit sharing)?	0	0	4	1	3	2.13
Do you feel appreciated by your supervisor/ management for a job well done?	1	1	3	3	0	3.00
SUBTOTAL	1	7	14	5	5	2.81
CATEGORY D: CORPORATE ENVIRONMENT						
Do you feel employees display teamwork and cooperation to reach a common goal?	0	3	2	3	0	3.00
Do you feel there is a friendly and upbeat atmosphere at work and high moral among all employees?	0	4	2	2	0	3.25

CONFIDENTIAL EMPLOYEE SURVEY COMPANY ABC			GROUP D - ENGINEERING				April 25, 2000			
No. in Group	10	No. Participating in Survey	8	% of Participation			80%			
RATING FACTOR				5	4	3	2	1		Average
CATEGORY D: CORPORATE ENVIRONMENT (continuation)										
Are you happy and proud of being part of the Company and believe in its successful future?				0	3	5	0	0		3.38
Do you feel the Company has enough social activities, such as luncheons, parties and picnics, to make it a pleasant work environment?				2	5	1	0	0		4.13
Is your work area clean & comfortable, well lit, and overall do you feel that the Company has a nice facility?				0	4	2	1	1		3.13
SUBTOTAL				2	19	12	6	1		3.38
CATEGORY E: COMPANY'S PERFORMANCE										
Are the Company's rules and procedures appropriate and fair?				0	3	2	3	0		3.00
Does the Company communicate goals and performance results to all employees?				0	3	2	2	0		3.25
Have you been provide with correct tools and support to perform your job effectively?				2	3	5	0	0		3.38
Do you feel there is emphasis on product quality and customer focus?				0	7	1	0	0		4.13
Have you received sufficient training, instructions and skill development to perform tasks efficiently?				0	3	2	1	1		3.13
SUBTOTAL				2	19	12	6	1		3.38
CATEGORY F: MANAGEMENT PERFORMANCE										
Are you confident that Management is doing a good job in creating a successful Company with a bright future?				0	4	4	0	0		3.50
Are you confidence that Management will do its best to protect the interest of the employees?				1	3	1	2	1		3.13
Is Management fair and supportive towards employees?				0	4	3	0	1		3.25
Does Management recognize and appreciate employees' efforts and performance?				1	1	4	2	0		3.13
Does Management provide sufficient motivation and incentive programs for employees?				0	2	3	3	0		2.88
SUBTOTAL				2	14	15	7	2		3.18
TOTALS				12	83	73	28	12		3.246

<u>Comments / Suggestions:</u> (enter in space below)

CONFIDENTIAL EMPLOYEE SURVEY COMPANY ABC	GROUP E - WEST COAST BRANCH				April 25, 2000	
No. in Group 8	**No. Participating in Survey** 8		**% of Participation**		**100%**	*Average*
RATING FACTOR	**5**	**4**	**3**	**2**	**1**	**Average**
CATEGORY A: PAY & BENEFITS						
How does your Income (salary) compare to similar jobs within the local area?	0	1	4	3	0	2.75
How do the company Benefits (Health, Dental, Disability, Life, Vacation, Holidays, etc.) compare to similar companies within the local area?	4	3	1	0	0	4.38
How do the Retirement Benefits (401K matching and profit sharing) compare to similar companies within the local area?	1	2	5	0	0	3.50
SUBTOTAL	5	6	10	3	0	3.54
CATEGORY B: JOB SATISFACTION						
Do you feel a sense of achievement and job accomplishment?	1	4	3	0	0	3.75
Do you feel you have the ability to provide input and influence decisions related to job performance?	2	2	4	0	0	3.75
Do you feel that your job is secure?	2	2	3	1	0	3.63
Are you able to take initiative and make improvements in job performance and work environment issues in the company?	3	1	3	1	0	3.75
SUBTOTAL	8	9	13	2	0	3.72
CATEGORY C: RECOGNITION AND PROMOTION						
Do you feel recognized and treated fairly by supervisors and the Company in general?	2	3	2	1	0	3.75
Do you feel that there is potential for internal promotions and career growth within the Company?	0	1	7	0	0	3.13
Do you feel that job performance and personal output is linked to reward (income, bonus and profit sharing)?	1	2	5	0	0	3.50
Do you feel appreciated by your supervisor/ management for a job well done?	2	2	3	1	0	3.63
SUBTOTAL	5	8	17	2	0	3.50
CATEGORY D: CORPORATE ENVIRONMENT						
Do you feel employees display teamwork and cooperation to reach a common goal?	0	4	3	1	0	3.38
Do you feel there is a friendly and upbeat atmosphere at work and high moral among all employees?	2	2	4	0	0	3.75

No. in Group	8	No. Participating in Survey	8	% of Participation		100%	

	RATING FACTOR	5	4	3	2	1	Average
CATEGORY D: CORPORATE ENVIRONMENT (continuation)							
Are you happy and proud of being part of the Company and believe in its successful future?		2	3	3	0	0	3.88
Do you feel the Company has enough social activities, such as luncheons, parties and picnics, to make it a pleasant work environment?		1	2	5	0	0	3.50
Is your work area clean & comfortable, well lit, and overall do you feel that the Company has a nice facility?		0	3	3	2	0	3.13
	SUBTOTAL	5	14	18	3	0	3.53
CATEGORY E: COMPANY'S PERFORMANCE							
Are the Company's rules and procedures appropriate and fair?		1	3	4	0	0	3.63
Does the Company communicate goals and performance results to all employees?		1	3	2	2	0	3.38
Have you been provide with correct tools and support to perform your job effectively?		1	2	3	2	0	3.25
Do you feel there is emphasis on product quality and customer focus?		2	2	4	0	0	3.75
Have you received sufficient training, instructions and skill development to perform tasks efficiently?		2	1	1	4	0	3.13
	SUBTOTAL	7	11	14	8	0	3.43
CATEGORY F: MANAGEMENT PERFORMANCE							
Are you confident that Management is doing a good job in creating a successful Company with a bright future?		1	3	4	0	0	3.63
Are you confidence that Management will do its best to protect the interest of the employees?		2	2	4	0	0	3.75
Is Management fair and supportive towards employees?		2	3	3	0	0	3.88
Does Management recognize and appreciate employees' efforts and performance?		2	2	4	0	0	3.75
Does Management provide sufficient motivation and incentive programs for employees?		1	1	4	1	1	3.00
	SUBTOTAL	8	11	19	1	1	3.60
	TOTALS	38	59	91	19	1	3.552

<u>Comments / Suggestions:</u> (enter in space below)

No. in Group	64	No. Participating in Survey	57	% of Participation		89%	

	Group A	Group B	Group C	Group D	Group E	Average
CATEGORY A: PAY & BENEFITS						
How does your Income (salary) compare to similar jobs within the local area?	2.28	2.56	3.00	2.25	2.75	2.57
How do the company Benefits (Health, Dental, Disability, Life, Vacation, Holidays, etc.) compare to similar companies within the local area?	2.68	3.56	3.00	3.38	4.38	3.40
How do the Retirement Benefits (401K matching and profit sharing) compare to similar companies within the local area?	3.04	4.33	3.86	3.38	3.50	3.62
SUBTOTAL	2.67	3.48	3.29	3.00	3.54	3.20
CATEGORY B: JOB SATISFACTION						
Do you feel a sense of achievement and job accomplishment?	3.04	2.89	3.29	3.88	3.75	3.37
Do you feel you have the ability to provide input and influence decisions related to job performance?	2.88	2.67	2.57	3.38	3.75	3.05
Do you feel that your job is secure?	3.32	3.89	3.29	3.50	3.63	3.52
Are you able to take initiative and make improvements in job performance and work environment issues in the company?	3.04	3.00	2.86	4.00	3.75	3.33
SUBTOTAL	3.07	3.11	3.00	3.69	3.72	3.32
CATEGORY C: RECOGNITION AND PROMOTION						
Do you feel recognized and treated fairly by supervisors and the Company in general?	2.72	3.22	3.29	3.38	3.75	3.27
Do you feel that there is potential for internal promotions and career growth within the Company?	2.72	2.56	2.86	2.75	3.13	2.80
Do you feel that job performance and personal output is linked to reward (income, bonus and profit sharing)?	2.80	2.67	2.86	2.13	3.50	2.79
Do you feel appreciated by your supervisor/ management for a job well done?	2.68	3.11	3.00	3.00	3.63	3.08
SUBTOTAL	2.73	2.89	3.00	2.81	3.50	2.99
CATEGORY D: CORPORATE ENVIRONMENT						
Do you feel employees display teamwork and cooperation to reach a common goal?	3.12	2.89	2.29	3.00	3.38	2.93
Do you feel there is a friendly and upbeat atmosphere at work and high moral among all employees?	3.08	3.22	3.14	3.25	3.75	3.29

No. in Group	64	No. Participating in Survey	57	% of Participation	89%

	Group A	Group B	Group C	Group D	Group E	Average
CATEGORY D: CORPORATE ENVIRONMENT (continuation)						
Are you happy and proud of being part of the Company and believe in its successful future?	3.32	3.22	3.14	3.38	3.88	3.39
Do you feel the Company has enough social activities, such as luncheons, parties and picnics, to make it a pleasant work environment?	4.32	4.44	3.57	4.13	3.50	3.99
Is your work area clean & comfortable, well lit, and overall do you feel that the Company has a nice facility?	3.46	4.33	3.14	3.13	3.13	3.44
SUBTOTAL	**3.46**	**3.62**	**3.06**	**3.38**	**3.53**	**3.41**
CATEGORY E: COMPANY'S PERFORMANCE						
Are the Company's rules and procedures appropriate and fair?	3.36	3.33	3.00	3.00	3.63	3.26
Does the Company communicate goals and performance results to all employees?	3.35	3.89	3.00	3.13	3.38	3.35
Have you been provide with correct tools and support to perform your job effectively?	3.12	3.78	2.86	3.88	3.25	3.38
Do you feel there is emphasis on product quality and customer focus?	3.28	3.44	3.00	3.88	3.75	3.47
Have you received sufficient training, instructions and skill development to perform tasks efficiently?	2.96	2.89	3.00	3.25	3.13	3.04
SUBTOTAL	**3.21**	**3.47**	**2.97**	**3.43**	**3.43**	**3.30**
CATEGORY F: MANAGEMENT PERFORMANCE						
Are you confident that Management is doing a good job in creating a successful Company with a bright future?	3.12	3.11	3.14	3.50	3.63	3.30
Are you confidence that Management will do its best to protect the interest of the employees?	3.32	3.11	3.29	3.13	3.75	3.32
Is Management fair and supportive towards employees?	2.92	3.22	3.29	3.25	3.88	3.31
Does Management recognize and appreciate employees' efforts and performance?	2.76	2.89	3.14	3.13	3.75	3.13
Does Management provide sufficient motivation and incentive programs for employees?	2.72	3.00	2.86	2.88	3.00	2.89
SUBTOTAL	**2.97**	**3.07**	**3.14**	**3.18**	**3.60**	**3.19**
TOTALS	**3.02**	**3.27**	**3.08**	**3.25**	**3.55**	**3.23**

Survey Index ⟋

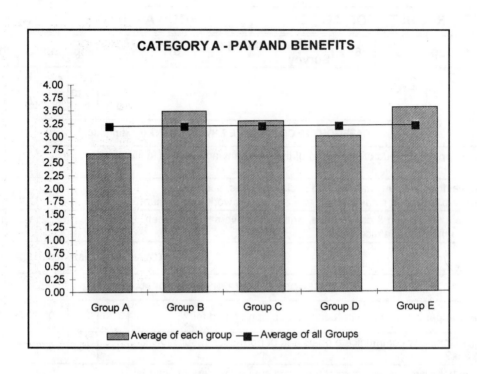

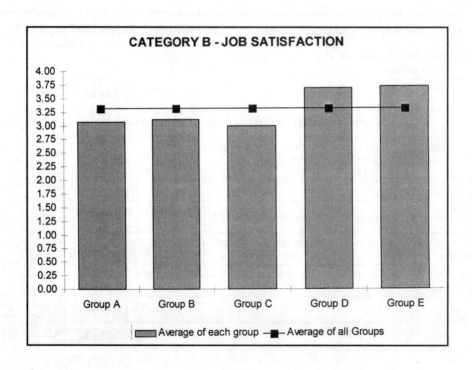

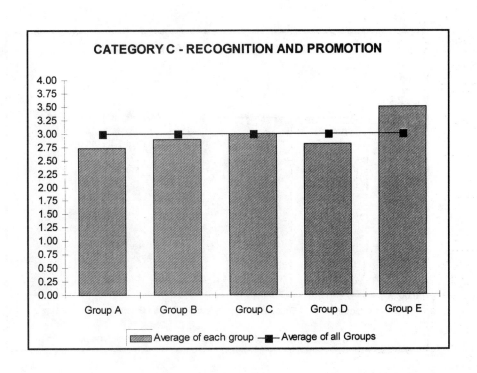

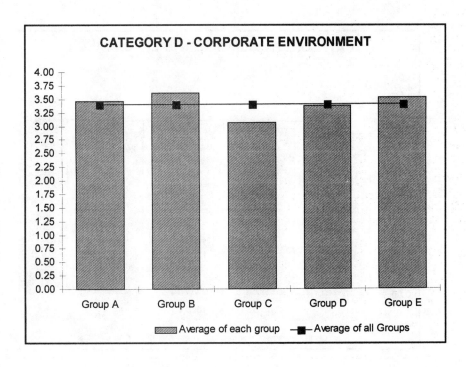

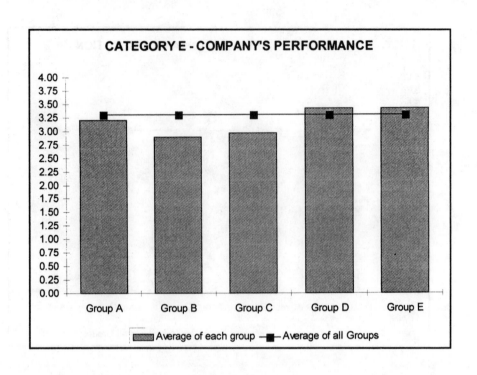

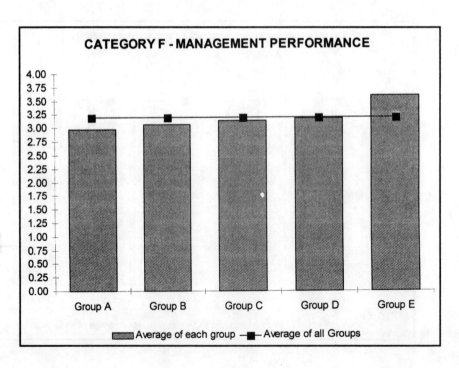

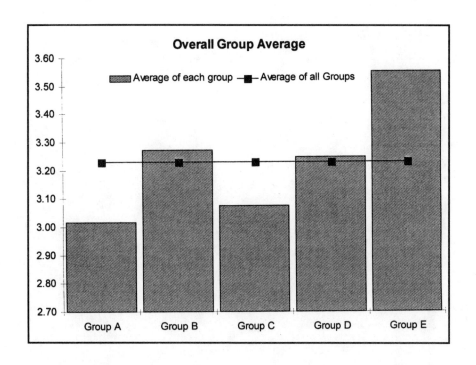

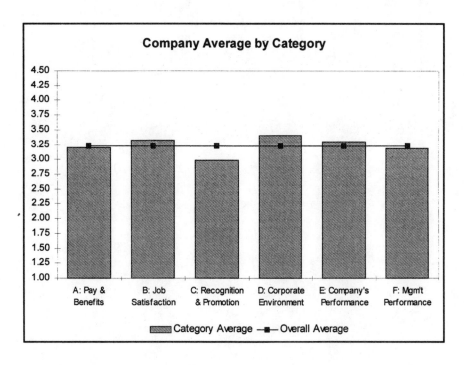

85

CHAPTER SEVEN
INCENTIVE PLAN IN ACTION

7.1 Employee Review Process

The employee review process will conform to the compensation schedule established at the onset of the plan, e.g. every three months.

The periodic review is generally short and concise. Group supervisors review each employee for the performance criteria and personal objectives selected for them (see Chapter 4). Ratings are assigned for each performance category and the percentage of completion is entered for the assigned tasks. Employees have the opportunity to provide feedback, comments, and suggestions to their supervisors during this review.

The Human Resources department can review the ratings and the employee's comments and approve them if they do not see any objectionable issues. The approved scores will become part of the employee's record and will be used in the calculation of the incentive compensation. See example on *page 90.*

7.2 Entering the Data

All other quantitative periodic results associated with the incentive factors and the compensation sources are entered into the program by the Finance department or as designated by company management. ***This process must be done in a timely manner to show management's commitment to the plan and to build employee trust.***

The Finance department ensures that all incentive factors are monitored continuously throughout the period, so that periodic results will be available ***on time***.

7.3 Employee Benefit Statements

When the data entry and calculation process is complete, employee bonus calculation statements are generated automatically by the program. See example on *page 91.*

The statement displays the following items:

a. Employee's applicable incentive factor goals and their allocated weight
b. Employee's performance and personal objective scores (where applicable).
c. Actual results obtained for each incentive factor, the percent of goal that was achieved, and the corresponding score (derived from the score tables).
d. Incentive pay calculation.
e. Incentive pay amount.

Summary data of incentive dollars earned for each compensation period is included from the second period onward. At the end of the year the annual statement will show the total amount of incentive pay earned for the year, last year's total (if any), and percentage variation from last year.

The program also generates a projected bonus report for each employee. This report displays the factor goals and their weight allocation, and assumes a score of 100 for each factor. The report also details compensation sources and their allocation; allowing employees to predict their incentive pay should they achieve a score of 100 in all their goals. See an example of this report on *page 92*.

7.4   Periodic Reports

Periodic and year-to-date reports are available for management's review and monitoring. A selected sample of these reports will be demonstrated in this section. For a complete list of reports available from the program refer to *pages 53-55.*

Periodic incentive payment reports are generated per employee, per group and for the entire company, with percentage changes from period to period. A brief description of these reports follows:

- Group Summary Report
  Displays the payout per compensation period for each individual in the group, the total payout per individual and for the group, and the percent of total each indi-

vidual received. Data from the prior year, if available, is also displayed and used to show percent variation from year to year. See example of report on *page 93*.

- Company Bonus Report
  Shows the incentive payout for each group in the company for every compensation period, the percent of total each group received, company totals to date, last year's totals (if available), and the percent variation from the previous year. See example of this report on *page 94*.

- Group Compensation Allocation
  Displays the percentage distribution of the compensation sources among the different groups participating in the plan. Compensation sources are analyzed in terms of projected revenue per source, maximum projected source allocation, and actual projected source allocation. See example of this report on *page 95*.

- Actual Compensation Allocation and Payout
  Portrays the incentive pay allocated to each group in the plan, the actual payout at the plan closing date, and the percent variation between the two. See example on *page 96*.

Other statistical data, reports, and graphics can be customized to management's requirements.

ABC Company
Personal Evaluation For Compensation Period Ending 9/30/2000

Administration, HR Supervisor
Employee Name: Walters, Jim   Emp. #: 5074
Job Description: Supervisor, HR
Supervisor Name: Brown, Joyce

Category Rating	Weight	Rating	Weighted	Performance Ratings:
A: Teamwork	10%	4	4.0	
C: Efforts	15%	5	8.0	5 Excellent
D: Dedication	15%	4	6.0	4 Very Good
G: Mentoring	20%	4	8.0	3 Acceptable
H: Conflict Management	20%	4	8.0	2 Marginal
I: Meeting Objectives	10%	4	4.0	1 Not Acceptable
J: Corrective Action	10%	4	4.0	

Total Possible Rating: 50   **Total Rating 41.5**

ABC Company
Personal Objectives For Compensation Schedule Ending 9/30/2000

Administration, HR Supervisor
Employee Name: Walters, Jim   Emp. #: 5074
Job Description: Supervisor, HR
Supervisor Name: Brown, Joyce

Objective	Priority	Difficulty	Due Date	Weight (W)	Completion (C)	W x C
Perform Annual HR Employee Review	1	7	07/15/2000	30%	100%	30%
Complete company wide training	2	8	08/01/2000	30%	95%	28.5%
Asses tools for Incentive Compensation Program	3	8	09/30/2000	40%	100%	40%
Totals		**22**		**100%**		**98.50%**

Percent Completed: 98.50%	Score (S): 88
Total Difficulty: 22	Score Adjustment (A): 110%
(Minimum Difficulty: 20)	Adjusted Score (S x A): 88 x 110% = 97

ABC Company
Bonus Calculation for Compensation Period 12/31/2000

Run Date: 01/05/2001

Administration, HR Director

Employee Name: Baker, Tom   Emp. No. 107
Job Description: Director, HR Department
Supervisor Name: Brown, Joyce

FACTOR	GOAL	ACTUAL	CALC.	SCORE (S)	FACTOR (F)	S x F
Budget (x$1000)	$ 27.50	$ 24.50	10%	190	30%	57.00
Cost Reduction (x$1000)	$ 27.50	$ 26.00	5%	100	30%	30.00
Personal Evaluation	50	45	45	105	20%	21.00
Personal Objectives	100%	100%	100%	115	20%	23.00
TOTAL (The total factor percentage must equal 100%)					**100.00%**	**131**
PERFORMANCE INDEX (PI)						**1.31**

COMPENSATION SOURCE	COMPENSATION VALUE	PERCENT ALLOCATION	SOURCE ALLOCATED
Earnings Per Share	$ 0.13	2,500 Shares	$ 325.00
Pre-Tax Earnings	$ 880,000.00	0.3000%	$ 2,640.00
		Total Compensation Source Allocated	**$ 2,965.00**

Period Bonus (PB) = Compensation Source (CS) x Performance Index (PI)

PB	=	CS	x	PI
$ 3,884.15		$ 2,965.00		1.31

PAYMENT AUTHORIZATION AND BONUS HISTORY FOR COMPENSATION PERIOD ENDING 12/31/2000

Bonus For: Baker, Tom
Date of Bonus Report: 1/16/2001

BONUS	3/31/2000	6/30/2000	9/30/2000	12/31/2000
	$ 2,227.35	$ 2,171.40	$ 3,784.50	$ 3,884.15

Total This Year: $ 12,067.40
Prior Year Total: $ 8,528.00
   % Variation: 29.3%

Title of Authorizer: CEO

ABC Company
Projected * Bonus Calculations (Excluding EPS)   Run Date: 11/16/2000
For Period Ending 12/31/2000

Executive: VP Engineering
        Employee Name: Chapman, Robert   Emp. No. 107
        Job Description: Engineering Manager
        Supervisor Name: Holland, Marie

FACTOR	GOAL	ACTUAL	CALC.	SCORE* (S)	FACTOR (F)	S x F
Budget (x$1000)	$ 275.00			100	10%	0.10
GPM	36%			100	20%	0.20
Quality Assurance	0			100	20%	0.20
Return on Investments	19%			100	25%	0.25
Sales Dollars (x1000)	$10,250.00			100	25%	0.25
TOTAL (The total factor percentage must equal 100%)					100.00%	1.00
				Performance Index (PI)		1.00

COMPENSATION SOURCE	COMPENSATION VALUE	PERCENT ALLOCATION	SOURCE ALLOCATED
Earnings Per Share	$ 0.00	(10,000 Shares)	$ 0.00
Total Stockholder Return (Dollars)	$ 275,000.00	0.3000%	$ 825.00
Economic Value Added (EVA)	$ 750,000.00	0.3000%	$ 2,250.00
EBIT	$ 850,000.00	0.3400%	$ 2,890.00
Total Compensation Source Allocated			$5,965.00

Period Bonus (PB) = Compensation Source (CS) x Performance Index (PI)

        PB   =   CS   x   (PI)
    $ 5,965.00 $ 5,965.00   1.00

* Projection assumes a score of 100 for each Factor

ABC Company
Group Bonus Summary for Group: Administration
Period: Year 2000

Run Date: 1/16/2001

Emp. ID	Employee Name	Subgroup	Bonus for Compensation Period:				Total This Year	% of Total	Total Last Year	% Variation
			3/31/2000	6/30/2000	9/31/2000	12/31/2000				
107	Baker, Tom	HR Director	$2,227.35	$2,171.40	$3,784.50	$3,884.15	$12,067.40	35.4%	$8,528.00	29.33%
5076	Boyd, Sue	HR Admin	$740.85	$750.20	$1,154.25	$1,204.95	$3,850.25	11.3%	$3,305.50	14.15%
5077	Chambers, Evelyn	HR Admin	$673.50	$750.20	$1,117.80	$1,204.95	$3,746.45	11.0%	$3,305.50	11.77%
5074	Walters, Jim	HR Supervisor	$1,621.80	$1,221.00	$2,158.00	$2,192.40	$7,193.20	21.1%	$5,884.00	18.20%
5075	Williams, Robert	HR Supervisor	$1621.80	$1,221.00	$2,224.40	$2,116.80	$7,184.00	21.1%	$5,884.00	18.10%
	Group Total		$6,885.30	$6,113.80	$10,438.95	$10,603.25	$34,041.30	100%	$26,907.00	20.96%

ABC Company
Company Bonus Report for Year 2000

Group	Total Bonus Per Compensation Period:				Total	Percent of Total	Total Last Year	% Variance
Administration	3/31/2000 $6,885.30	6/30/2000 $6,113.80	9/31/2000 $10,438.95	12/31/2000 $10,603.25	$34,041.30	4.5%	$26,907.00	20.96%
Engineering	3/31/2000 $32,105.48	6/30/2000 $27,026.67	9/31/2000 $30,971.00	12/31/2000 $35,152.28	$125,255.43	16.7%	$101,167.32	19.23%
Executive	3/31/2000 $48,059.93	6/30/2000 $42,806.29	9/31/2000 $43,649.79	12/31/2000 $50,344.75	$184,860.76	24.7%	$148,972.67	19.41%
Finance	3/31/2000 $15,512.16	6/30/2000 $14,751.17	9/31/2000 $19,771.15	12/31/2000 $20,880.47	$70,914.95	9.5%	$57,634.43	18.73%
Quality Assurance	3/31/2000 $8,333.42	6/30/2000 $7,786.34	9/31/2000 $8,531.20	12/31/2000 $10,560.30	$35,211.26	4.7%	$29,609.24	15.91%
Sales	1/31/2000 $22,086.12; 7/31/2000 $21,347.75	2/29/2000 $23,786.97; 8/30/2000 $14,703.47	3/31/2000 $28,638.60; 9/30/2000 $26,768.13	4/30/2000 $22,329.56; 10/31/2000 $26,510.48	5/31/2000 $23,865.89; 11/30/2000 $30,996.84	6/30/2000 $26,787.27; 12/31/2000 $30,334.49	$298,155.57	39.9%	$238,213.84	20.11%
Total					**$748,439.27**	**100%**	**$602,504.50**	**19.5%**

ABC Company
Group Compensation Allocation Report, Plan Year 2000

Run Date: 1/05/2000

Group / Source	Administration	Engineering	Executive	Finance	Quality Assurance	Sales	Total
EBIT			2.9950% / 3.00%	0.9700% / 1.00%			3.9650% / 4.00%
Economic Value Added (EVA)		1.9600% / 2.00%	1.7500% / 2.00%	0.9700% / 1.00%			4.6800% / 5.00%
Pre-Tax Earnings	1.0000% / 1.00%	1.9600% / 2.00%			0.9500% / 1.00%		3.9100% / 4.00%
Sales Dollars						0.800% / 1.00%	0.8000% / 1.00%
Total Stockholder Return (Dollars)			1.8000% / 2.00%	0.9700% / 1.00%			2.7700% / 3.00%

Actual Allocation Percentages (Top Row)
Group Pre-allocated (or Maximum) Percentages (Bottom Row)

Source	Projected Source Revenue	Projected Max% Allocation	Projected Source Allocation (Max)	Actual % Allocation	Projected Source Allocation (Actual)
EBIT	$ 3,200,000.00	4.00%	$ 128,000.00	3.9100%	$ 125,120.00
Economic Value Added (EVA)	$ 35,000,000.00	1.00%	$ 350,000.00	0.8000%	$ 280,000.00
Pre-Tax Earnings	$ 2,300,000.00	5.00%	$ 115,000.00	4.6800%	$ 107,640.00
Sales Dollars	$ 3,400,000.00	4.00%	$ 136,000.00	3.9650%	$ 134,810.00
Total Stockholder Return (Dollars)	$ 1,200,000.00	3.00%	$ 36,000.00	2.7700%	$ 33,240.00
Total			**$765,000.00**		**$680,810.00**

ABC Company
Company Actual Compensation Allocation and Payout   **Run Date: 1/16/2001**
Period: Year 2000

Group Name	Allocated Incentive Pay[1]	Percent of Total	Actual Payout[2]	Percent of Total	Percent Variation
Administration	$32,000.00	4.70%	$34,041.30	4.55%	6.38%
Engineering	$107,800.00	15.83%	$125,255.43	16.73%	16.19%
Executive	$163,680.00	24.04%	$184,860.76	24.70%	12.94%
Finance	$66,930.00	9.83%	$70,914.95	9.48%	5.95%
Quality Assurance	$30,400.00	4.47%	$35,211.26	4.70%	5.83%
Sales	$280,000.00	41.13%	$298,155.57	39.84%	6.48%
Total	$680,810.00	100.00%	$748,439.27	100.00%	9.93%

Note 1 – Excluding EPS Allocation
Note 2 – Includes EPS Allocation if Utilized

7.5 Assessing Progress and Success of Plan

At the conclusion of each quarter, it is strongly recommended that management review the progress of the plan to ensure its objectives are being met. Several issues must be examined closely:

a.   Were company goals met?
b.   Were employees rewarded adequately?
c.   Are morale, productivity, and profitability on the rise?

Figure 7.5 on *page 97* is a flowchart of the management review process. It demonstrates how a quick analysis can provide management with feedback on plan progress and identify problem areas. On occasion, problem areas are isolated to a specific group rather than the whole company. In such cases, attention should be focused on refining the plan for problem areas only, while functioning groups continue on the same plan.

FIGURE 7.5 PERIODIC MANAGEMENT REVIEW

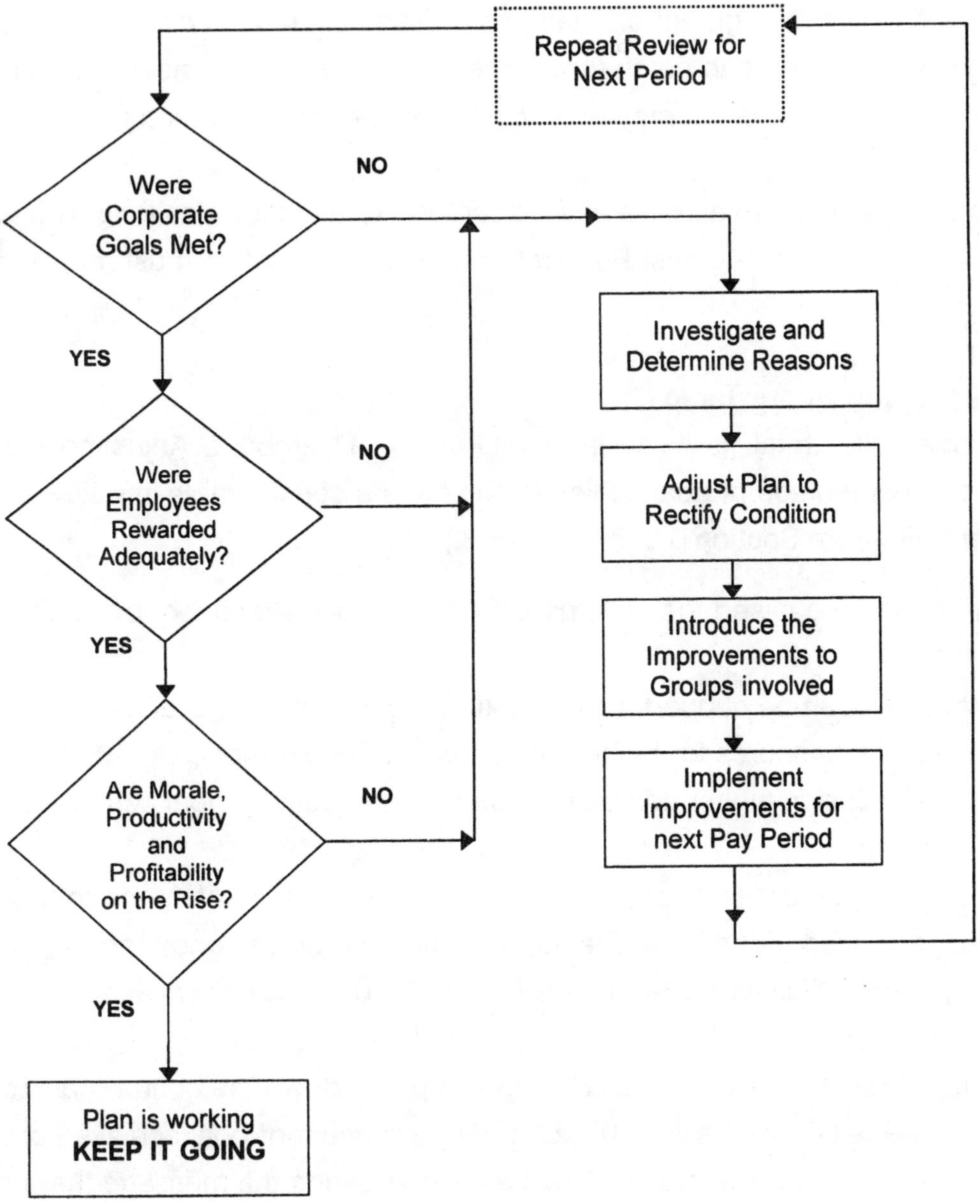

7.6 Adjusting Plan Toward Reaching Objectives

The plan emphasizes *total flexibility for adjustment* so changes may be made easily. Adjustments can be made in several areas.

7.6.1 Adjusting the Weight Allocated to Incentive Factors

You may discover that an initial percentage allocation to a certain incentive factor is ineffective due to misjudgment or changing conditions. In such cases, the percentage originally allocated can be changed, the allocation from an incentive factor can be removed, or an allocation may be added to a new incentive factor.

There is total flexibility to allocate any percentage to any factor as long as it is effective in reaching company goals. Remember that total allocation must remain 100 percent.

7.6.2 Adjusting Score Tables

Score tables offer total flexibility in adjusting benefit amount. Adjusting the scores assigned to percentage of goal achieved can have a considerable impact on employee benefit. (Refer to Section 3.8 in Chapter 3.)

a. If the scores are raised, benefits rise. If the scores are reduced, benefits decline.

b. Score tables can be capped with a maximum percent of goal achieved or can be assigned higher scores for higher percentages. For example, cap at 150 percent or continue to assign higher scores to higher percentages of goal achieved.

c. The 100 point score level can be adjusted up or down in reference to the percent of goal achieved. For example, a score of 100 can be assigned for 90 percent of goal achieved or assign the same score to 100 percent of goal achieved, etc.

d. The threshold "zero" score can be moved up and down the bonus scale to impact benefit. For example, assign "0" score for 50 percent of goal achieved or raise it to 70 percent of goal achieved. Such a change sends the message that achieving below 70 percent of goal is *unacceptable*.

e. Adding smaller increments to percentage of goals achieved and their corresponding scores will also create an increase in the benefit. For example, if a line is
added to the percent of goal achieved column on table 3.8 on *page 31*, at 98
percent and a score of 108 is assigned, the benefit will have a marginal increase
if an employee reaches the 98 percent level. (The way it is set up there is no
increase in score between 95 percent and 100 percent.)

7.6.3 Adjusting Compensation Sources and Allocation

Compensation sources can be added or deleted as necessary (refer to sections 3.9
and 3.10 in Chapter 3) and the percent of each compensation source allocated to
groups, subgroups, and employees can be adjusted.

Such changes can have considerable impact on the incentive dollars each employee
earns. Use caution when adjusting compensation sources and their allocation
downward. Have a solid justification for doing so to avoid a negative impact on
employee morale and loyalty.

CHAPTER EIGHT
MEASURING THE SUCCESS OF THE INCENTIVE COMPENSATION PROGRAM

Companies that invest a lot of time, effort, and resources into an incentive compensation program want to be able to measure the progress and success of the plan. This can be accomplished by using measurement tools, which will assess the results obtained in business performance areas that are ***directly influenced by the program***.

Figure 8.1 on *page 102* is a flowchart of the steps in the process of measuring the success of the program. Each step will be explained in detail in this chapter.

8.1 Step 1 – Determine Business Performance Categories to be Measured

Incentive programs have specific goals and reasons for their implementation and are expected to yield certain benefits targeted by the program. By reviewing these goals and reasons carefully, we can determine the main business performance areas that are expected to improve as a result of implementing the program.

Such areas may include:

     a. Financial Measures

     b. Workforce Measures

     c. Productivity Measures

     d. Business Improvement Measures

     e. Customer Measures

     f. Vendor Measures

     g. Cost Reduction Measures, etc.

Figure 8.1 Measuring the Success of the Incentive Compensation Program

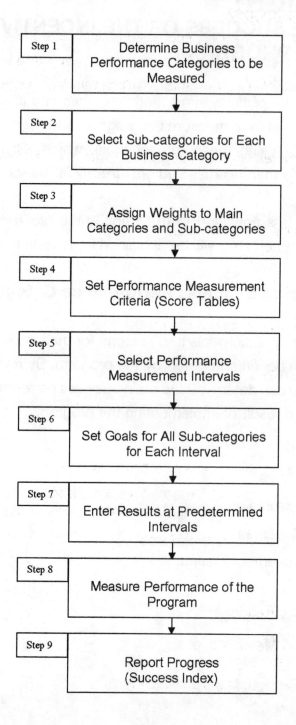

Step 1 — Determine Business Performance Categories to be Measured

Step 2 — Select Sub-categories for Each Business Category

Step 3 — Assign Weights to Main Categories and Sub-categories

Step 4 — Set Performance Measurement Criteria (Score Tables)

Step 5 — Select Performance Measurement Intervals

Step 6 — Set Goals for All Sub-categories for Each Interval

Step 7 — Enter Results at Predetermined Intervals

Step 8 — Measure Performance of the Program

Step 9 — Report Progress (Success Index)

8.2 Step 2 – Determine Sub-categories for Each Business Performance Category

Each business category is subdivided into specific sub-categories that will be measured for performance results obtained at the end of each interval. Sub-categories selected must have an established method by which they will be measured at the end of each interval.

Following are some examples of sub-categories, (note that all should be attributable to the incentive program):

A. Financial Measures

Return on Investment

Earning Growth

Earnings per Share

EBIT (Earning Before Interest and Taxes)

B. Workforce Measures

Employee Morale

Job Satisfaction

Employee Retention Rate

Ability to attract new talent (Ease of recruitment)

$$\text{e.g. Hire Rate} = \frac{\text{No. of New Employees Hired}}{\text{No. of Firm Job Offers}} = \frac{12}{20} = 60\%$$

Approval of Management by Workforce

Employee Loyalty

C. Productivity Measures

Increase in Production Yield

Product Quality Improvement

Improvement in Product Development Cycle

D.   Business Improvement Measures

Increase Revenue

Growth Rate

Growth in Value of Intellectual Property

Increase in Gross Profit Margin

New Business Development

E.   Customer Measures

On-time Delivery (Products and/or Services)

Quality Improvement (Products and/or Services)

Customer Satisfaction

Customer Retention Rate

New Customer Acquisition Rate

[= Bids Won/Qualified Bids Submitted]

F.   Vendor Measures

Vendor Quality Rate

Vendor On-time Delivery Rate

Vendor Price-reduction Rate

Vendor Loyalty

G.   Cost Reduction Measures

Cost Reduction in Operating Expenses

Cost Reduction in Production Materials

Cost Reduction in Supplies

Cost Reduction in Recruitment

8.3   Step 3 – Assign Weights

In reviewing the main business performance categories, determine the weight or importance each main category plays in the total measurement process. Assign weights to the main categories first and, then, using the same analysis process, distribute the weight assigned to the main categories into the sub-categories.

8.4   Step 4 – Set Performance Measurement Criteria (Score Tables)

Score tables are the elements through which the performance criteria for each business performance sub-category is established. The score represents the performance level achieved by the company on each business performance sub-category. A score table consists of three main elements:

- **threshold** the minimum level of performance that must be obtained in each business performance category considered acceptable by the company.
- **ceiling** the highest performance level that can be obtained in a specific business performance category.
- **increment** the steps at which the business performance rating will vary, e.g. the category can be stepped up every 1%, 2%, 3%, 4%, or 5% of goal achieved.

Table 8.4 on *page 106* is an example of a score table. This table shows the score the company will obtain if they reach anywhere between 75 percent and 125 percent of the goal for a specific business performance category.

A score of 100 points is obtained if the percent of goal achieved for *increase in revenue* reaches 90 percent. The score is higher as higher percentages of the goal are reached. Achieving below 80 percent of goal nullifies the score in this sub-category. In this particular example, the measurements are made in 5 percent increments; however, score tables are flexible and can be set according to each company's needs.

Table 8.4 Score Table for Increase in Revenue Goal

% of Sales Goal Achieved	Score
125%	150
120%	140
115%	130
110%	120
105%	115
100%	110
95%	105
90%	100
85%	90
Below 80%	0

Threshold = 80%, Ceiling = 125%, Increment = 5%

8.5   Step 5 – Select Measurement Interval

Decide when and how often you want to track the progress of the plan's success. Normally, a quarterly measurement interval is sufficient. More or less frequent intervals may be established, as long as the data for business performance results is available.

8.6   Step 6 – Set Goals for all Sub-categories for Each Interval

All the business sub-categories selected to be used in the index should have specific targets or goals. These goals will become the benchmark for comparison at the end of every interval.

8.7   Step 7 – Enter Results at Predetermined Intervals

At the end of each measurement interval, the actual results obtained for each business sub-category will be finalized and entered into the program. Such results are obtained from the business enterprise software or other programs used for reporting results on key business benchmarks.

8.8   Step 8 – Measure Performance of the Program

By comparing the results to the goals, a percent of goal achieved can be determined. To each level of percent of goal achieved, a score will be assigned based on the performance criteria established in Step 4 (score tables).

The cumulative sum of scores multiplied by the weights in all the business subcategories selected will yield the **success index**.

The success index is designed to be 100 percent if all goals are met. If goals were exceeded, the Index will be above 100 and if goals are not met, the index will be below 100.

8.9   Step 9 – Report Progress

By comparing the success index at subsequent intervals we can monitor the progress and trend of the success of the program. In addition, reviewing the score levels in each sub-category can identify problem areas.

Identifying problem areas will trigger a review of the program as it relates to the specific non-performing categories and sub-categories. For example, a score below 80 in any sub-category can be considered inadequate and flagged for additional analysis. Corrective action can be initiated to improve non-performing areas and maximize their contribution to the program's success.

Figure 8.9 on *page 108* is an example of a success index plotted over time.

Figure 8.9   Success Index for Co. ABC

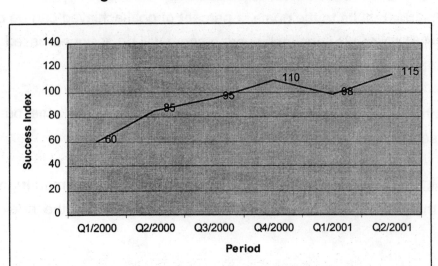

8.10 An Example of Incentive Compensation Program Success Index

Several measurement categories and sub-categories can be utilized and combined to assess the success of the program. Each sub-category will have its own target goal and a score table where the performance criteria for that specific sub-category will be defined (refer to Step 4).

In the example shown in Figure 8.10 A, four main categories and corresponding weights have been selected in obtaining the success index.

Figure 8.10 A   Business Performance Categories for ABC Co.

Business Performance Categories	Weight (%)
Financial Measures	30
Workforce Measures	30
Customer Measures	20
Cost Reduction Measures	20
Total Weight	**100%**

Each category is further subdivided into specific sub-categories and the total category weight is distributed between the sub-categories according to how critical they are to the program's success.

The sub-category goals are derived from the company's strategic business plan, which has to be finalized before the program is put in place. Clearly the incentive compensation program is being set to accomplish certain objectives. These objectives have to be documented, quantified, and communicated to all the participants in the program. Figure 8.10 B on *page 110* demonstrates an example of how these categories and sub-categories can be combined to obtain the success index.

An example of the score table for Return on Investment sub-category is shown in figure 8.10 C below. Using the same method, score tables are set up for each sub-category.

Figure 8.10 C   Score Table for Return on Investment

Return on Investment (%)	Score
25 and Above	150
24	140
23	130
22	120
21	110
20 Goal	100
19	90
18	75
17	60
16	50
Below 16	0

Figure 8.10 B Incentive Compensation Program Success Index for Company ABC

Period: Q1, 2000   Date: April 2, 2000

Business Categories	Category Weight	Sub-Category	Weight (W)	Goal	Actual	Score (S)	Weighted Score (S) x (W)
Financial Measures	30%	Return on Investment	8%	20%	22%	120	9.6
		Earnings Per Share	8%	$ 0.25	$ 0.28	115	9.2
		Pre-Tax Earnings	7%	$ 2.5M	$ 2.9M	130	9.1
		Growth in Revenue	7%	18%	16%	85	5.95
		Subtotal	30%	--	--	--	33.85
Workforce Measures	30%	Job Satisfaction	8%	95%	98%	130	10.4
		Employee Retention Rate	8%	92%	93%	110	8.8
		Recruitment of New Talent (Hire Rate)	7%	60%	63%	115	8.05
		Management Approval Rate	7%	95%	92%	80	5.6
		Subtotal	30%	--	--	--	32.85
Customer Measures	20%	Customer Retention Rate	7%	90%	92%	115	8.05
		Customer Satisfaction Rate	6%	95%	94%	90	5.4
		Customer Acquisition Rate	7%	50%	55%	130	9.1
		Subtotal	20%	--	--	--	22.55
Cost Reduction Measures	20%	Cost Reduction in Operating Expense	8%	$ 200K	$ 140K	60	4.8
		Cost Reduction in Supplies	5%	$ 50K	$ 40K	75	3.75
		Cost Reduction in Material Cost	7%	$ 60K	$ 55K	85	5.95
		Subtotal	20%	--	--	--	14.5
						Success Index	103.75

CHAPTER NINE
HOW TO REWARD YOUR EMPLOYEES

9.1 Introduction

Your incentive compensation plan will generate the amount of reward dollars earned by each participant in the plan. These award dollars can be defined in three ways:

(i) Cash Dollars, which are to be paid to the participant in cash through the company's payroll

(ii) Reward Dollars, which can be used via a commercial provider network that the company has established relationships with for shopping, travel, entertainment, etc.

(iii) Reward Points, where each dollar equals a point, which can be used in the same manner the reward dollars are used.

9.2 Cash vs. Non-cash Rewards

The debate regarding the advantages and disadvantages of cash rewards versus non-cash rewards has existed for years. Valid arguments support both sides of the controversy. What is clear is that cash rewards are most likely to be perceived as entitlement, just like another paycheck, which may lead to creating a weak link between the employee's achievement and the reward. Employees who receive cash rewards will most often use it for non-emotional purposes such as paying bills, buying groceries, etc., and the residual emotional value of the reward and its source (the company) becomes minimal.

Employees may perceive a cash reward as a pay-cut if the same amount of cash does not appear the next compensation period, and this may generate resentment and low morale. Employees may also feel that they do not need to put forth the extra effort to earn the cash incentive because it blends with their regular compensation.

On the other hand, non-cash rewards such as family vacations, merchandise items, concert tickets, etc., have a strong emotional and social value for the employee and are easily associated with their achievement and the company. These rewards have a pleasant, tangible, and memorable value for the recipient that is shared with their family members and friends. They foster loyalty and long-term commitment to the organization.

9.3   Flexibility and the Buying Power of the Internet

Certainly, employees have different needs and priorities. As a result, companies have to exercise some flexibility in the way they administer the reward fulfillment to employees.

Some employees may have an urgent need for cash due to mounting debt or family emergencies while others may enjoy the comfort of using their earned rewards on pleasurable and memorable items. In the end, people work for what they can purchase with their earnings and if their company maximizes their buying power, they will be grateful and appreciative.

The technology revolution and the power of the Internet provide employers with more flexibility in the way they can allow employees to spend awards. Today virtually anything on the Internet can be bought using a credit card account. This means that if a company can facilitate an Internet connection (which is likely already in place) and a credit card account for employees, they may spend their reward dollars to their heart's content.

Nonetheless, it is essential to maintain a strong emotional attachment between the provider (the company) and the user (the employee) so that the link between the reward and the source is always evident.

In order to allow flexibility in the manner of which the rewards are used the company can set guidelines on how rewards can be allocated between the expenditure categories offered by the company.

9.4 Award Allocation

The company can create and select several categories in which employees may spend their award dollars.

9.4.1 Contribution into Retirement Plans (401K)

First and foremost, in order to make sure that employees are saving enough for their retirement, the company can require employees who do not meet a minimum level of contribution into retirement plans (say 5 percent of their salary), to contribute a certain portion of their incentive award dollars into such plans.

By promoting retirement contributions for employees who are ignoring their future needs, the company plays an important role in securing the comfortable retirement of its employees while reducing the mounting pressures on the Social Security system.

Employees will enjoy an investment that grows exponentially over the years for the following reasons:
a) their contribution is paid by the company from their reward dollars
b) their contribution is tax free (pre-tax dollars)
c) the company will match a portion of their contribution according to its 401K plan rules
d) the investment will grow tax deferred until retirement age

9.4.2 Company Stock

Secondly, the company may recommend their employees designate a percentage of the incentive dollars (say 10 percent) to be spent on buying company stock at a preferred price. This should be done only if the company executives believe that it is a sound, long-term investment for the employees.

9.4.3 Cash Component of Reward

The company may allow a certain portion of the incentive dollars, say 30 to 50 percent, to be taken by employees in cash, if they wish to do so, or leave it in their reward account to be used on goods and services. Employees, who need more cash due to personal reasons, can make special requests to increase the cash portion of their incentive dollars cash payout.

9.4.4 Non-cash Component of Reward

The balance of incentive dollars left in the employee account can be spent with provider network set up by the company via the Internet or by other means that the company chooses.

Table 9.1 on *page 115* is an example of an Employee Bonus Account Allocation and Expenditure module that allows the allocation and tracking of the incentive pay through several usage categories such as: cash, travel, merchandise, 401K contribution, company stock purchase, investment in securities, etc. This module can track all usage categories and account balances for individuals.

Table 9.2 on *page 115* is an example of an Account Allocation and Expenditure report for the entire company.

Table 9.1   Employee Bonus Account Allocation and Expenditure

Employee Name:		Compensation Period:								
Group:		Subgroup:								

Employee Bonus Account Allocation & Expenditure Table

Bonus Paid	Q1 $1000		Q2 $1000		Q3 ---		Q4 $1000		Total $3000	
Bonus Allocation	% Allocated	$	% Allocated	$	% Allocated	$	% Allocated	$	% Allocated	$
Cash	30%	$300	30%	$300	---	---	---	---		$600
Investments in Securities	20%	$200	20%	$200	---	---	30%	$300		$700
401K Plan Contribution	20%	$200	10%	$100	---	---	30%	$300		$600
Merchandise	10%	$100	20%	$200	---	---	20%	$200		$500
Travel	10%	$100	20%	$200	---	---	20%	$200		$500
Company Stock Purchase Plan	10%	$100	---	---	---	---	---	---		$100
Total	100%	1000	100%	1000	0		100%	1000	3000	

Table 9.2   Employee Bonus Account Allocation and Expenditure for Company ABC

Company Bonus Account Allocation & Expenditure Table for Period: Q1/2000

Account Category	Group A	Group B	Group C	Group D	Total	% of Total
Cash	10K	5K	5K	10K	30K	25.4%
Investments in Securities	8K	3K	5K	5K	21K	17.8%
401K Plan Contribution	4K	5K	5K	10K	24K	20.3%
Merchandise	5K	3K	2K	5K	15K	12.7%
Travel	5K	3K	3K	3K	14K	11.9%
Stock Purchase Plan	4K	3K	2K	4K	14K	11.9%
Total	36K	22K	22K	38K	118K	100%
% of Total	30.5%	18.64%	18.64%	32.22%	100%	

CHAPTER TEN
SAMPLE PLANS FOR CORPORATIONS AND INDIVIDUALS

10.1   Sample of a Corporate Incentive Compensation Plan

This section provides an example for a corporate incentive compensation plan document that can be used as a template for any company adopting a new incentive compensation program.

Use this template as you see fit in the design and implementation of your own incentive compensation plan, and make changes as needed.

INCENTIVE COMPENSATION PLAN
FOR ABC CORP.

Revision No. _____   Date: _____

CONFIDENTIAL

1.   INTRODUCTION

This Incentive Compensation Plan is intended to provide employees with a periodic compensation pay based on the following three elements:

1) Meeting the Corporate Goals

2) Individual and Group performance

3) Corporate profitability

This plan sets forth the guidelines and formulas for the computation of compensation payments for participating ABC employees. Compensation calculations will be made according to the compensation schedule established in the plan. Payments for each compensation period will be made to eligible employees within 30 days of the last day of such compensation period. All compensation payout computed under this plan are subject to final approval and modification by the president and/or CEO of ABC. This plan may be modified or withdrawn at any time without prior notice at the sole discretion of the president and/or CEO of ABC Corporation.

Eligible employees are full-time ABC Corp. employees who are selected to participate in the plan, are employed by ABC during the entire compensation period for which the incentive is being paid, and are on ABC's payroll at the time the compensation payout is issued.

2. PLAN PRINCIPLES

The plan will be operated on the following principles:

a) Set the Goals

The company will set the corporate and individual's goals on a periodic basis and revise them as needed.

b) Measure Performance

The company will measure its performance and the performance of the individuals on its plan at the end of each compensation period.

c) Reward

The company will reward the employees according to the measured results at the end of the compensation period.

3. PLAN STRUCTURE

3.1 The plan is based on several **incentive factors** (commonly called business goals) that have been determined as critical to the company's success in achieving its strategic objectives.

3.2 Employees are divided into **employee groups** and **subgroups**, which are similar in job function.

3.3 **Incentive factors** are assigned to the employee groups that have responsibility, control, or influence over them.

3.4 Once the incentive factors have been assigned to each group, the subgroups within each group are examined carefully to determine which incentive factors are most relevant to the subgroup and the importance these factors play within the subgroup in relation to reaching the set goals. Based on this determination, **factor weights** are assigned to the incentive factors selected for the subgroup. The total factor weight allocated to every subgroup should equal 100 percent. Weight is not allocated to every incentive factor assigned to the group, only to those the subgroup should focus on achieving.

4. INCENTIVE FACTORS

The following incentive factors have been selected for use in this plan. Management has established goals for each one of these incentive factors as shown in Table 4.0 below.

4.1 Corporate Sales Goals

4.2 Gross Profit Margin (GPM)

4.3 New Product Development

4.4 Cost Reduction Efforts

4.5 Increase Customer Satisfaction

4.6 Controlling Budget

4.7 Personal Performance Evaluation

4.8 Personal Objectives

Table 4.0 Company's Business Goals

ABC Corporation Three Year Strategic Business Goals				
Corporate Goals	Current Year	**Year 1**	Year 2	Year 3
Achieve Corporate Sales	5M	**10M**	20M	40M
Improve Gross Profit Margin	34%	**36%**	38%	40%
Development of New Product Lines	2	**4**	6	8
Obtain Cost Reduction	N/A	**250K**	500K	750K
Control Budget	2M	**4M**	8M	12M
Increase Customer Satisfaction	95%	**96%**	98%	99%

4.1 Corporate Sales Goals

Corporate sales goals are set at the beginning of every year. At the end of every measurement period, *actual* sales figures are compared to the sales goals and the percent of goal achieved is determined. A corresponding score is assigned to each level of percent of goal achieved.

According to table 4.1, employees are entitled to a score of 100 points if they reach 100 percent of the goal. The score is higher as higher percentages of the goal are reached. The minimum level of acceptable performance (threshold) is 70 percent. Measurements are made in 5 percent increments.

The score table established for Incentive Factor *Sales* is shown below.

Table 4.1   Score Table for Sales Goals

% OF GOAL ACHIEVED	SCORE (POINTS)
150%	160
145%	155
140%	150
135%	145
130%	140
125%	135
120%	130
115%	125
110%	120
105%	110
100%	100
95%	90
90%	80
85%	70
80%	60
75%	40
70%	30
LESS THAN 70%	0

Threshold = 70%, Ceiling = 150%, Increment = 5%

Example: % of Goals Achieved $= \dfrac{\text{Actual Sales}}{\text{Sales Goals}} = \dfrac{5.0M}{4.0M} = 125\%$

➢ 125% corresponds to a score of 135 points.

NOTE: For percentages that fall in between, refer to lower figures and scores, (i.e., if 117% is achieved, refer to 115% and 125 score).

4.2   Gross Profit Margin (GPM) Goals

GPM is defined as sales minus cost of goods sold. This is the company's gross profit before expenses.

Gross profit margin goals are set from historical data related to the company's past performance or from related industry benchmarks. The historical average will usually entitle the employee to a score of 100 points. Increased GPM will entitle employees to higher scores.

The score table established for Incentive Factor *Gross Profit Margin* is shown in Table 4.2 below.

Table 4.2   Score Table for GPM Goals

GPM % ACHIEVED	SCORE (POINTS)
46% AND ABOVE	200
45%	190
44%	180
43%	170
42%	160
41%	150
40%	140
39%	130
38%	120
37%	110
36% (HISTORICAL AVERAGE)	100
35%	80
34%	60
33%	40
32%	20
LESS THAN 32%	0

Threshold = 32%, Ceiling = 42%, Increment = 1%

4.3   New Product Development

Management has established goals for developing new product in accordance with the company's marketing strategy and customer demand.

At the end of each measurement period, the number of actual product lines developed is compared to the goal. A percent of goal achieved is determined and a corresponding score is assigned. Table 4.3 on *page 123* shows the score table for Incentive Factor *Product Development*.

Table 4.3 Score Table for Product Development Goals

% OF GOAL ACHIEVED	SCORE (POINTS)
125%	155
120%	146
115%	137
110%	128
105%	119
100%	110
95%	95
90%	80
85%	65
80%	50

Threshold = 80%, Ceiling = 125%, Increment = 5%

4.4   Cost Reduction Efforts

This section applies to cost reduction efforts in all company operations. Cost reduction is defined as reducing in operating expenses on any product, service or process used by the company. Cost reduction could be external, such as obtaining reduced prices from vendors and service providers or internal, by improving the efficiency of internal operations.

Management has established cost reduction goals for all departments at the beginning of the fiscal year. The goal has been set as a percentage of present operating cost, e.g. reduce operating costs by 5 percent.

Each department manager will keep records of cost reduction efforts using the Cost Reduction Approval form, see example on *page 126*. Cost savings are totaled at the end of each compensation period and submitted to the Accounting department by each department manager. Total cost savings will be compared to previous operating costs and the percentage of cost reduction can be derived as follows:

$$\% \text{ of cost reduction } = \frac{\text{Total Cost Saving}}{\text{Previous Operating Expenses}}$$

$$\text{Example: } \% \text{ of cost saving } = \frac{10,000}{200,000} = 5\%$$

In order to track the cost reduction efforts, a simple spreadsheet program can be setup to automate the cost reduction calculations. See example of form on *page 126*.

Score table 4.4 established for *Cost Reduction* is shown below.

Table 4.4   Score Table for Cost Reduction Goals

% OF COST REDUCTION	SCORE
10% & above	150
9%	140
8%	130
7%	120
6%	110
5%	100
4%	80
3%	50
2%	30
1%	20
Stay within Projected Costs	0

Threshold = 1%, Ceiling = 10%, Increment = 1%

4.5   Increase Customer Satisfaction

Score table 4.5 established for *Increasing Customer Satisfaction* is shown below,

Table 4.5   Score Table for Customer Satisfaction Goals

% OF CUSTOMER SATISFACTION	SCORE
100%	180
99%	160
98%	140
97%	125
96% (GOAL)	100
95% (HISTORICAL AVERAGE)	80
94%	40
93%	20
BELOW 93%	0

Threshold = 93%, Ceiling = 100%, Increment = 1%

4.6   Controlling Budget

This factor will measure how the company's operating budget is controlled.

Scores will depend on whether actual spending is above or below the approved budget. Calculations will relate to the current fiscal budget approved by the corporation.

Score table 4.6 established for *Budget Control* is shown below.

Table 4.6   Score Table for Budget Goals

DESCRIPTION	SCORE
Kept expenses 10% below budget	150
Kept expenses 9% below budget	140
Kept expenses 8% below budget	130
Kept expenses 7% below budget	120
Kept expenses 6% below budget	110
Kept expenses 5% below budget	100
Kept expenses 4% below budget	85
Kept expenses 3% below budget	70
Kept expenses 2% below budget	50
Kept expenses 1% below budget	30
Kept expenses within budget	20
Overspent budget without authorization	0

Threshold = 1%, Ceiling = 10%, Increment = 1%

COST REDUCTION APPROVAL FORM

EMPLOYEE NAME: _____   EMP.#_____

DEPARTMENT: _____   REF. NO.:_____

COMMODITY, SERVICE OR ACTIVITY:

_____

PREVIOUS/PROJECTED COST:_____

DATE:_____

NEW/ACTUAL COST:_____   DATE:_____

TOTAL SAVINGS:_____

APPROVED BY:_____

SUPERVISOR'S NAME:_____   DATE:_____

COST REDUCTION SPREADSHEET FORM

DEPARTMENT: _____   YEAR: _____

Date	Cost Reduction Category	Employee No.	Ref. No.	Q1	Q2	Q3	Q4	TOTAL
Total Savings ($)								
Previous Operating Expenses								
% of Cost Reduction								

$ SAVED

4.7   Employee Personal Performance

Employees who will be assessed using the performance evaluation incentive factor, will be assigned between five to 10 performance categories that will focus their efforts on those skills and abilities critical to their job function.

4.7.1 Performance Categories

Performance evaluation will be measured using any of the following 10 predefined categories:

A. *Motivation* – Reflects the employee's desire and drive to carry out the job in a productive, creative, and cheerful manner, displaying a positive attitude and strong sense of achievement.

B. *Problem Solving* – Reflects the employee's ability to identify a problem, analyze it, generate potential solutions to eliminate it and select the solution that is most effective and least expensive.

C. *Effort* – Measures extra efforts put forth by the employee to ensure that duties and assigned tasks are accomplished in a satisfactory manner.

D. *Efficiency* – Measures the degree of effectiveness at performing daily functions and special assignments maximizing the utilization of available resources.

E. *Accuracy* – Measures the employee's ability to perform daily duties in an error-free manner, displaying exactitude and thoroughness at each task.

F. *Follow Up* – Reflects on the manner in which the employee follows up on:
    (a) Tasks that have to be accomplished on a regular basis.
    (b) Instructions and or directions given to them by their superiors.
    (c) Instructions and/or directions given by them to other employees under their supervision.

G. *Teamwork* – Measures the ability of working and coordinating overall efforts with other departments or team members, thus ensuring a fast and smooth flow of information. The emphasis is on overall corporate team efforts and working in harmony with others toward reaching the company's goals.

H. *Meeting Objectives* – Evaluates the ability of the employee to accomplish objectives determined by management and/or specific tasks that have been assigned by supervisors.

I. *Corrective Action* – Measures the responsiveness of the employee to correct problems or deficiencies that have occurred in the past and improve in areas where performance enhancement is required (as pointed out in reviews, verbal, and written communications).

J. *Flexibility* – Reflects on the employee's adaptability to changes due to organizational growth and the capacity to adjust priorities on a moment's notice without falling into disorder and confusion.

4.7.2 Performance Category Weights

A weight has been allocated for each performance category selected for an employee based on the importance such category plays in the employee's performance of the job function. The cumulative weight allocated to each employee must equal 100 percent.

Table 4.7.2 shows an example of five performance categories and their allocated weights:

Table 4.7.2 Performance Categories and Weight Allocation

Performance Category	Weight Allocated
Problem-Solving Skills	25%
Effort	20%
Corrective Action	20%
Efficiency	20%
Teamwork	15%
Total Weight	**100%**

4.7.3 Rating System

A rating system has been established so that managers and supervisors assessing employees' performance use a standard evaluation scale. The following performance key will be used:

$$5 = \text{Excellent}$$
$$4 = \text{Very good}$$
$$3 = \text{Acceptable}$$
$$2 = \text{Marginal}$$
$$1 = \text{Unacceptable}$$

0.5 increment can be used for in between scores, e.g. 2.5, 3.5, etc.

4.7.4 Performance Evaluation Score Tables

The score table defines the achievement level expected from the employee. The score represents the percent of the incentive that the employee will receive depending on the rating they obtain. Higher levels of achievement will yield higher scores and consequently increased incentive payout.

Score table 4.7.4 has been established for performance evaluation as shown below.

Table 4.7.4 Performance Evaluation Score Table

TOTAL POINTS	SCORE
LESS THAN 35	0
35	60
37	80
40	90
43	100
45	110
47	130
MAXIMUM 50	150

NOTE: Maximum rating is 50, minimum rating is 35. A rating below 35 will nullify the portion of the incentive allocated to this factor.

4.7.5 End of Period Review

At the end of each compensation period, the manager or immediate supervisor will meet with each employee and conduct a review of his or her performance on-line. A rating will be assigned to each selected performance category and the employee will have the opportunity provide feedback, comments, and/or suggestions.

Table 4.7.5 shows an example of the weighted-rating obtained for each performance category. The cumulative weighted-rating for all categories equals 40.5.

Table 4.7.5   Rating and Weighted-rating by Category

Performance	Weight Allocated	Rating	Weighted Rating
Problem-solving Skills	25%	4.5	11.25
Effort	20%	4.0	8.0
Corrective Action	20%	4.0	8.0
Efficiency	20%	4.0	8.0
Teamwork	15%	3.5	5.25
		Cumulative Weighted-rating	40.50
		Score *	90

* Looking at the Performance Evaluation Score Table (Table 4.7.4 on *page 129*), the score corresponding to a weighted-rating of 40.50 is 90, which means that the employee will receive 90 percent of the incentive allocated to this factor.

4.8   Personal Objectives

Employees that will be measured using the personal objective incentive factor will be assigned several tasks, projects, jobs, or goals by their supervisors or managers, to be completed within a compensation period.

4.8.1 Assigning Objectives

a) Supervisors or managers will ensure each objective is described in explicit detail so the employee can understand clearly what is expected to be accomplished.

b) The manager or supervisor will specify the "deliverables" that will be obtained by the employee at the completion of the task. Deliverables may be reports, proto-types, certifications, etc.

c) A "difficulty level" on a scale from one to 10 (1 = easiest, 10 = hardest) will be assigned for each task or objective. This component measures the relative degree of complexity involved in completing the task.

d) When more than one objective is assigned, the supervisor or manager will determine the priority of each task.

e) Each task is allocated a weight. The weight determines the relative importance of the tasks in relation to the other tasks assigned for the same period. The total weight assigned to all the tasks must equal 100 percent.

f) Finally, each task is assigned a date by which it should be completed.

Table 4.8.1 shows an example of personal objectives assignments.

Table 4.8.1 Personal Objectives

Employee Name:		Period:		
Group:				
Objective	Difficulty Level	Priority	Due Date	Weight
Obtain ISO Registration	9	1	1/30/2000	40%
Implement Contractor Performance Rating	8	2	2/28/2000	35%
Prepare Annual Review for Board	8	3	3/31/2000	25%
Total	24			100%

4.8.2 Personal Objectives Score Table

The score table defines the achievement level expected from the employee. Higher levels of completion of personal objectives will yield higher scores and increased incentive. Score table 4.8.2 established for personal objectives is shown below.

Table 4.8.2 Personal Objectives Score Table

% OF COMPLETION	SCORE
(Min.) 80%	54
85%	65
90%	77
95%	88
(Max.) 100%	100

Threshold = 80%, Ceiling = 100%, Increment = 5%

4.8.3 Difficulty Booster

In order to be fair to employees who are assigned several tasks with a combined difficulty level higher than the minimum required, their scores will be boosted to reflect the added effort put forth to complete these projects.

First, a minimum combined difficulty level must be set for all participants using personal objectives, so that everyone receives a fair allocation of the work.

Employees who are assigned higher than the minimum difficulty level will benefit from boosted scores depending on the total difficulty assigned to them and how well they completed the assignments.

Table 4.8.3 on *page 133* shows how scores will be adjusted to reflect the employee's added effort in performing the job.

Table 4.8.3 Personal Objectives Score Adjustment Table

Total Difficulty Level	Score Adjustment %
20 (Min. level that must be assigned)	100%
22	110%
24	120%
26	130%
28	140%
30	150%
32	160%
34	170%
36	180%
38	190%
40 (Max. Difficulty Level)	200%

Threshold = 20%, Ceiling = 40%, Increment = 2%

4.8.4 End of Period Review

At the end of each compensation period, the group manager or supervisor meets with the employee and reviews the final progress on all the assigned objectives.

Based on this review, a percent of completion will be entered for each objective. Depending on the number of objectives and their respective weights, a cumulative percentage of objective completion will be established for the combined tasks assigned for that period.

Table 4.8.4 on *page 134* shows an example of the personal objectives data and cumulative completion at the end of the compensation period.

Table 4.8.4 End of Period Review of Personal Objective Factor

Employee Name:					Period:	
Group:						
Objective	Difficulty Level	Priority	Due Date	Weight	% Completion	Weighted Completion
Obtain ISO Registration	9	1	1/30	40%	100	40%
Implement Contractor Performance Rating	8	2	2/28	35%	100	35%
Prepare Annual Review for Board	8	3	3/31	25%	90	22.5%
Totals	24			100%		97.5%
					Score	88
					Adjusted Score	106*

* Adjusted Score = Score (88) x Score Adjustment (120%) = 106

5. ASSIGNING INCENTIVE FACTORS TO GROUPS

Incentive factors are assigned to the groups and subgroups that have responsibility, control, and influence over them. Plan participants should constantly be reviewing these factors and their goals, monitoring their progress and adjusting their priority to meet their goals. Incentive factor goals serve as constant reminders as to which area employees should focus their efforts.

The following table shows the incentive factors assigned to each corporate group.

Table 5.0   Incentive Factors Assigned per Group for Company ABC

Incentive Factors	Groups				
	Executive	Software Development	Operations	Sales/ Mktg	Finance/ Administration
Sales Dollar	✓	✓		✓	
GPM (%)	✓		✓	✓	
Cost Reduction	✓		✓		✓
Product Development	✓	✓			
Budget	✓	✓	✓		✓
Customer Satisfaction	✓	✓	✓	✓	✓
Performance Evaluation			✓		✓
Personal Objectives		✓	✓		✓

Table 6.0   Incentive Factor Weight Allocation by Subgroup

Group	Subgroup	% of Factor Allocation to the Subgroup Level								
		Sales	GPM	Produc Devel.	Cost Reduct	Budget	Cust. Satisf.	Emplo Evalua	Person Object.	Total Weight
Executive (3)	CEO	30	20	15	10	10	15	--	--	100%
	President	40	20	20	--	--	20	--	--	100%
	QA Manager	25	--	25	25	--	25	--	--	100%
Software Development (3)	Software Development Mgr.	30	--	50	--	10	10	--	--	100%
	Configuration Mgmt Engineer	25	--	45	--	10	10	--	10	100%
	Program Engineer	30	--	50	--	10	--	--	10	100%
Operations (4)	Operations Manager	25	25	--	25	25	--	--	--	100%
	Technical Support Specialist	30	15	--	25	15	--	15	--	100%
	Shipping/Receiving Clerk	50	--	--	20	--	--	15	15	100%
	Buyer	--	25	--	50	--	--	--	25	100%
Sales and Marketing (5)	Director, Sales and Marketing	50	35	--	--	--	15	--	--	100%
	Sales Exec. Region A	60	30	--	--	--	10	--	--	100%
	Sales Exec. Region B	60	30	--	--	--	10	--	--	100%
Finance / Admin. (5)	CFO	25	25	--	25	25	--	--	--	100%
	Accountant	--	--	--	30	30	10	10	20	100%
	Comptroller	--	--	--	30	30	10	10	20	100%
	Administrative Staff	--	--	--	20	20	10	20	30	100%

6. ALLOCATING INCENTIVE FACTORS AND WEIGHTS TO SUB GROUPS

The incentive factors assigned to each group were examined carefully to determine which factors should be allocated to the subgroup level. Subgroups were allocated the incentive factors they have the most influence on and control over. These will now be the focal point of the subgroup's efforts.

Next, a weight is distributed among the factors assigned to each subgroup based on the importance each factor plays within the subgroup in relation to reaching the set goals. The factor weight is the percentage of the factor allocated to a specific subgroup. The total factor weight for each subgroup should equal 100 percent.

Table 6.0 on *page 135* shows the factor weight distribution for the subgroups of ABC Corp.

7. COMPENSATION SCHEDULE

The compensation schedule is the period during which the goal attainment progress will be measured and the incentive payment will be calculated. At the end of the compensation period, comparing the incentive factor goal to the actual performance is the key factor in determining incentive compensation pay.

Compensation schedules have been established for a monthly, quarterly, and semi-annual distribution as indicated in Table 7.0.

Table 7.0   Compensation Schedule for each Group

Groups	Compensation Schedule			
	Monthly	Quarterly	Semi-annually	Annually
Executive			✓	
Engineering		✓		
Operations		✓		
Sales & Marketing	✓			
Finance/Admin		✓		

8. COMPENSATION SOURCES

The compensation sources are the financial resources through which the incentive plan will be funded. ABC Corp. has established the financial goals shown in Table 8.0 to be achieved in the current year.

Table 8.0   ABC Corp. Financial Goals

Financial Goals	Projected Revenue
Pre-Tax Profit	$ 1,000,000
Cost Reduction	$ 250,000
Earnings Per Share	$ 0.60
Return on Capital	25%
Stockholder Equity	$ 4,200,000

The company selected two compensation sources to fund the plan. A percentage of the selected compensation sources will be used to fund the plan as shown in Table 8.1.

Table 8.1   Compensation Sources and Percent Allocated to the Plan

Compensation Sources	Projected Source Revenue	% Allocated	Projected Source Allocation
Pre-Tax Profit	1,000,000	15%	150K
Cost Reduction	250,000	50%	125K
Total Projected Source Allocated			225K

9. ALLOCATION OF COMPENSATION SOURCES

Compensation source allocation is defined as the percentage of the compensation source assigned to each group, subgroup, and employee. It is one of the key elements in determining the bonus amount employees will receive at the end of every compensation period.

This information is confidential and will be disclosed to each plan participant in a private manner. Group directors will *only have access* to the compensation source allocation data pertaining to their groups.

The percentage of pre-tax profit allocated for each subgroup in ABC Corp. is shown in Table 9.1 below. The percentage of allocation of Cost Reduction dollars is shown in Table 9.2 on *page 139*.

Table 9.1   Pre-Tax Profit Allocation by Subgroup

Group	Sub-Group	# of Employees in Subgroup	% of Profit Allocation per Employee	% of Profit Allocation per Subgroup	% of Profit Allocation per Group
Executive	CEO	1	1.5	1.5	3.75
	President	1	1.5	1.5	
	QA Manager	1	.75	.75	
Software Develop.	Software Development Mgr.	1	.75	.75	1.75
	Configuration Mgmt. Engineer	1	.5	.5	
	Program Engineer	1	.5	.5	
Operations	Operations Manager	1	.75	.75	2.05
	Technical Support Specialist	1	.5	.5	
	Shipping/Receiving Clerk	1	.4	.4	
	Buyer	1	.4	.4	
Sales & Marketing	Director, Sales and Marketing	1	1.2	1.2	4.2
	Sales Executive, Region A	2	.75	1.5	
	Sales Executive, Region B	2	.75	1.5	
Finance/ Admin.	CFO	1	1.5	1.5	3.55
	Administrative Staff	2	.4	.8	
	Accountant	1	.5	.5	
	Comptroller	1	.75	.75	
Number of Employees: 20			**Total Profit Allocation: 15.30%**		

Table 9.2   Cost Reduction Allocation by Subgroup

Group	Sub-Group	# of Employees in Subgroup	% Allocation per Employee	% Allocation per Subgroup	% Allocation per Group
Executive	CEO	1	3.0	3.0	9.0
	President	1	3.0	3.0	
	QA Manager	1	3.0	3.0	
Software Develop.	Software Development Mgr.	1	3.0	3.0	7.0
	Configuration Mgmt. Engineer	1	2.0	2.0	
	Program Engineer	1	2.0	2.0	
Operations	Operations Manager	1	3.0	3.0	10.0
	Technical Support Specialist	1	2.0	2.0	
	Shipping/Receiving Clerk	1	2.0	2.0	
	Buyer	1	3.0	3.0	
Sales & Marketing	Director, Sales and Marketing	1	3.0	3.0	9.0
	Sales Executive, Region A	2	1.5	3.0	
	Sales Executive, Region B	2	1.5	3.0	
Finance/ Admin.	CFO	1	5.0	5.0	15.0
	Administrative Staff	2	2.0	4.0	
	Accountant	1	3.0	3.0	
	Comptroller	1	3.0	3.0	
	Number of Employees: 20			**Total Allocation: 50.0%**	

10.   COMPENSATION CALCULATION METHOD

10.1   The Performance Index

The employee's performance in each incentive factor allocated is measured at the end of each compensation period. A score is assigned for each factor based on the actual results achieved for that period. The employee score in each factor category is multiplied by the factor weight allocated to it and divided by 100. Adding all factor category scores times their weights yields the Performance Index (PI).

The performance index is a cumulative index that represents the overall employee performance in achieving the assigned goals. The performance index reflects how well employees have achieved their goals in their respective incentive factors.

The performance index is derived using the following formula:

$$PI = \frac{S1 \times F1}{100} + \frac{S2 \times F2}{100} + \frac{S3 \times F3}{100} + \cdots\cdots \frac{S_n \times F_n}{100}$$

(Performance Index)

Where S1, S2, S3... etc., are scores achieved for each Incentive Factor.

F1, F2, F3... etc., are the weights allocated to the above factors respectively.

Note that F1+ F2+ F3+...+Fn = 100%.

10.2 The Compensation Pie (CP)

Each person participating in the plan is allocated a certain slice of the pie. The value of this pie is determined by adding the values of each compensation source selected for that person times the percent of the allocated source.

$$CP = CS_1 \times SA_1 + CS_2 \times SA_2 + CS_3 \times SA_3 + \ldots CS_n \times SA_n$$

(Compensation Pie)

Where CS_1, CS_2, CS_3 ... etc. are the compensation sources.

SA_1, SA_2, SA_3 ... etc. are the percentages allocated to each source respectively.

10.3 The Final Bonus

The final bonus is calculated as follows:

$$PB = PI \times CP$$

(Periodic Bonus) (Performance Index) (Compensation Pie)

Each employee participating in the plan will receive a two-page bonus statement summarizing performance, scores, and bonus calculations. Periodic bonus calculations will be based on cumulative year-to-date figures. Losses will be carried forward to offset gains in subsequent periods.

Bonus calculations will be made periodically as stated in the compensation schedule.

Bonus payments will be made to eligible employees within 30 days of the ending date of the last compensation period.

The company may reserve the right to make adjustments to bonuses paid for the last quarter of each year, should there be considerable changes made to the company's financial statements by the accounting firm auditing the company's annual financial records. Such adjustments can be made in the first quarter of the following year.

Sky is the limit...

Stay on firm ground...

Stick to your goals!

10.2   Samples of Individual Incentive Compensation Plans

The following incentive plan examples are tailored for individual positions within the company. Companies often find a need for more specific plans for certain positions within the company to better define their goals and maximize the performance of the individuals.

First, select the incentive factors that this individual has the most influence over as part of his job function. One or more incentive factors may be selected. Allocate weight for each factor selected according to the importance factors play in achieving the desired outcome.

Then, test a few hypothetical scenarios to make sure compensation payments match desired outcome. For example, if compensation payment increases corporate profitability increases. Avoid creating situations where individuals' benefits increase while corporate profitability stagnates or declines.

In this section, three samples of individual plans were created to demonstrate how such plans are put together.

- Section A—Plan for Operations Manager
- Section B—Plan for Sales Manager
- Section C—Plan for Office Manager

ABC CORP. INCENTIVE COMPENSATION PLAN FOR OPERATIONS MANAGER (OM)

JANUARY 2000
CONFIDENTIAL

1. INTRODUCTION

This Incentive Compensation Plan is intended to provide the operations manager (OM) with a quarterly incentive pay based on the following three key factors:

1. Meeting the Corporation's Production Goals
2. Meeting the Corporation's Cost Reduction Goals
3. Improving Product Quality (ISO9000)

Payments will be made within 30 days of the quarter ending date provided that the OM was fully employed by ABC Corp. for the whole quarter.

2. PLAN PRINCIPLES

The plan will be operated on the following principles:

a) Set the Goals

The company will set the corporate and OM's goals on an annual basis and revise them as needed.

b) Measure Performance

The company will measure its performance and the OM's performance on a quarterly basis.

c) Reward

The company will reward the OM on a quarterly basis depending on the measured results at the end of the compensation period.

3. PLAN STRUCTURE

3.1 The plan is based on the three **incentive factors** mentioned in section 1, which have been determined as critical to the company's growth and profitability.

3.2 OM is designated a **factor weight** for each of the incentive factors assigned to his job function. The weight allocation reflects the importance these factors play in achieving the goals. The total percentage allocated for all incentive factors is 100 percent.

4. INCENTIVE FACTORS

The following incentive factors are used in the plan:

4.1 Corporate Production Goals

The corporate production goals are set at the beginning of every year. The production goals for ABC Corp. for fiscal year 2000 are as follows:

Table 4.1.1 Production Goals for Operations Department
Fiscal Year 2000

Period	Number of Units
Q1	900
Q2	1,000
Q3	1,200
Q4	1,000
Total	4,100

At the end of every quarter, the *actual* number of production units is compared to the production goal and the percent of goal achieved is determined. A corresponding score is assigned to the level of percent of goal achieved. See Table 4.1.2 on *page 145*.

Table 4.1.2   Score Table for Production Goals

% OF GOAL ACHIEVED	SCORE (POINTS)
150% and above	175
145%	165
140%	160
135%	150
130%	145
125%	140
120%	130
115%	125
110%	120
105%	110
100%	100
95%	95
90%	90
85%	70
80%	50
LESS THAN 80%	0

Threshold = 80%, Ceiling = 150%, Increment = 5%

Example: % of Goal Achieved $= \dfrac{\text{Actual \# of Units Produced}}{\text{Goal of Units to be Produced}} = \dfrac{1200}{1100} = 109\%$

➤ 109% corresponds to a score of 110 points.

NOTE: For percentages that fall in between, refer to lower figures and scores (i.e., if* 109% is achieved, refer to 105% and 110 score).

4.2   Cost Reduction Goals

Cost reduction goals are set at the beginning of the year for each functional unit or department. Cost reduction goals for the Operations department of ABC Corp. for fiscal year 2000 are shown in Table 4.2.1:

Table 4.2.1 Cost Reduction Goals, Operations Department

Q1	Q2	Q3	Q4	Total
$ 100,000	$ 110,000	$ 120,000	$ 100,000	$ 430,000

At the end of the quarter, the *actual* cost reduction achieved is compared to the goal and a percent of goal achieved is determined. A corresponding score is assigned to the level of percent of goal achieved using the cost reduction score table shown below

Table 4.2.2   Score Table for Cost Reduction Goal

COST REDUCTION ACHIEVED %	SCORE (POINTS)
150%	180
140%	160
130%	150
120%	140
110%	130
100%	110
90%	100
80%	90
70%	70
60%	50
50%	40
Below 50%	0

Threshold = 50, Ceiling = 150%, Increment = 10%

4.3   Improving Product Quality and Compliance with ISO9000 Goals

The Operations department will be audited regularly by internal and external auditors to verify compliance with the ISO9000 Quality System. The ultimate goal of the Operations department is to have zero non-compliance and maintain a defect-free production line. Non-compliance can be recorded from either internal or external audits. Table 4.3 shows levels of non-compliance with corresponding scores

Table 4.3   Score Table for ISO 9000 Goals

% OF GOALS ACHIEVED	SCORE (POINTS)
Audit completed without non-compliance	150
Audit completed with one minor non-compliance	120
Audit completed with two minor non-compliance	90
Audit completed with three to four minor non-compliance	70
Audit completed with five minor non-compliance	30
Audit completed with one or more major non-compliance	0

5. WEIGHT ALLOCATION OF INCENTIVE FACTORS TO OM

Job Description	Factor Weight Allocation (F)		
	Production (F1)	Cost Reduction (F2)	Quality (F3)
Operations Manager	60%	20%	20%

6. INCENTIVE PAY CALCULATION METHOD

The OM score in each incentive factor category is multiplied by the factor weight allocated to it and divided by 100 percent. Adding all category scores times their factor weights yields the Performance Index (PI).

If the OM achieves a combined score of more than 100 points his bonus will be higher.

The performance index (PI) is derived using the following formula:

$$\text{PI (Performance Index)} = \frac{S1 \times F1}{100} + \frac{S2 \times F2}{100} + \frac{S3 \times F3}{100}$$

Where S1, S2, S3 are scores achieved for the incentive factors and F1, F2, F3 are weights allocated to each factor respectively.
Note that F1+F2+F3 = 100%

The final quarterly bonus is calculated as follows:

$$\textbf{QB} \text{ (Quarterly Bonus)} = \textbf{PI} \text{ (Performance Index)} \times \textbf{CP} \text{ (Compensation Pie)}$$

Where:

PI = Performance Index
CP = Compensation Pie

The compensation pie for the OM will consist of the following two elements:

Compensation Source	Allocation
Pre-tax Profits	0.50 %
Cost Reduction	1.5 %

OM will receive a quarterly bonus statement per attached example.

The company reserves the right to make changes or adjustments to this incentive pay plan without any notice.

7.   EXAMPLE OF QUARTERLY BONUS CALCULATION

7.1   Incentive Factors Actual Results

For the period of Q1/2000 the following results were reported for the incentive factors allocated to the operations manager:

Period Q1/2000

Incentive Factor	Goal	Actual	% Achieved	Score (S)	Factor (F)	S x F
Production	900	1020	113%	120	60%	72
Cost Reduction	100,000	80,000	80%	90	20%	18
Quality	0	1	------	120	20%	24
Total Score						114
PI (Peformance Index)			114 / 100 =			1.14

7.2   Compensation Source Actual Results

The following results were reported on the compensation sources:

Compensation Source	Q1/2000 Results	Allocation	Total
Pre-tax Profit	$ 250,000	0.50 %	$ 1,250
Cost Reduction	$ 80,000	1.5 %	$ 1,200
Total Compensation Source			$ 2,450

148

7.3   Quarterly Bonus Calculation

QB   =   PI   x   CP
(Quarterly   (Performance   (Compensation
Bonus)   Index)   Pie)

QB   =   1.14   x   2,450   = $ 2,793.00

ABC CORP. INCENTIVE COMPENSATION PLAN FOR SALES MANAGER (SM)

JANUARY 2000

CONFIDENTIAL

1.　INTRODUCTION

This Incentive Compensation Plan is intended to provide the sales manager (SM) with a monthly incentive pay based on the following three key factors:

1. Meeting the Corporation's Sales Goals
2. Meeting the Corporation's Order Booking Goals
3. Improving the Profit Margin of the Corporation

Payments will be made within 15 days from the last day of the previous month. Incentive pay is made only for months in which the SM has been fully employed with the company. For example, if the SM starts working during the middle of a month, the incentive plan will be in effect at the beginning of the following month.

2.　PLAN PRINCIPLES

The plan will be operated on the following principles:

a) Set the Goals

The company will set the corporate and SM's goals on an annual basis and revise them as needed.

b) Measure Performance

The company will measure its performance and the SM's performance on a monthly basis.

c) Reward

The company will reward the SM on a monthly basis depending on the measured results at the end of the compensation period.

3. PLAN STRUCTURE

3.1 The plan is based on the three **incentive factors** mentioned in section 1, which have been determined as critical to the company's growth.

3.2 SM is designated a **factor weight** for each of the incentive factors assigned to his job function. The weight allocation depends on how important a role these factors play in achieving the goals. The total percentage allocated for all incentive factors is 100 percent.

4. INCENTIVE FACTORS

The following incentive factors are used in the plan:

4.1 Corporate Sales Goals

The corporate sales goals are set at the beginning of every year.

The sales and booking goals for ABC Corp. for the fiscal year 2000 are shown on Table 4.1.1 below

Table 4.1.1 Sales and Booking Goals for Sales Department

Fiscal Year 2000

Month	Sales Goals $		Booking Goals $	
	Monthly	Cumulative	Monthly	Cumulative
January	800,000		850,000	
February	800,000	1,600,000	850,000	$1,900,000
March	825,000	2,425,000	875,000	2,775,000
April	850,000	3,275,000	900,000	3,675,000
May	875,000	4,150,000	900,000	4,575,000
June	900,000	5,050,000	950,000	5,525,000
July	850,000	5,900,000	900,000	6,425,000
August	850,000	6,750,000	900,000	7,325,000
September	900,000	7,650,000	975,000	8,300,000
October	950,000	8,600,000	1,000,000	9,300,000
November	950,000	9,550,000	1,050,000	10,350,000
December	1,000,000	10,550,000	1,100,000	11,450,000

At the end of every month, *actual* sales figures are compared to the sales goals and the percent of goal achieved is determined. A corresponding score is assigned to the level of percent of goal achieved. See Table 4.1.2 below.

Table 4.1.2 Score Table for Sales Goals

% OF GOAL ACHIEVED	SCORE (POINTS)
170% and above	200
160%	190
150%	180
140%	170
135%	160
130%	150
125%	145
120%	135
115%	125
110%	120
105%	110
100%	100
95%	90
90%	75
85%	60
80%	50
75%	40
LESS THAN 75%	

Threshold = 75%, Ceiling = 170%, Increment = 5%

Example: % of Goals Achieved $= \dfrac{\text{Actual Sales}}{\text{Sales Goals}} = \dfrac{5.0M}{4.0M} = 125\%$

➤ 125% corresponds to a score of 145 points.

NOTE: For percentages that fall in between, refer to lower figures and scores (i.e., if 117% is achieved, refer to 115% and 125 score).

4.2   Corporate Order Booking Goals

Order booking goals are targets set by the company for order receipts from its customers. The corporate order booking goals are set at the beginning of the year. The booking goals for ABC Corp. for the fiscal year 2000 are shown in Table 4.1.1 on *page 151.*

At the end of every month, *actual* bookings are compared to the goals and the percent of goal achieved can be determined. A corresponding score is assigned to the level of percent of goal achieved using Table 4.3 below,

Table 4.3 Score Table for Order Booking Goals

% OF GOALS ACHIEVED	SCORE (POINTS)
160%	200
155%	190
150%	180
145%	170
140%	160
135%	150
130%	140
125%	135
120%	130
115%	125
110%	120
105%	110
100%	100
95%	90
90%	85
85%	75
80%	65
75%	50
70%	40
Less than 70%	0

Threshold = 70%, Ceiling = 160%, Increment = 5%

Example: % of Goal Achieved $= \dfrac{\text{Actual Booking}}{\text{Booking Goals}} = \dfrac{4.8M}{4.0M} = 120\%$

➣ 120% corresponds to a score of 130 points.

NOTE: For percentages that fall in between, refer to lower figures and scores (i.e., if 117% is achieved, refer to 115% and 125 score).

4.3 Gross Profit Margin (GPM) Goals
GPM is defined as sales minus cost of goods sold.

Gross profit margin goals are set from historical data related to the company's past performance or from related industry benchmarks. The historical average will usually entitle the SM to a score of 100 points. Increased GPM entitles SM to higher scores. An example of GPM score table is shown below (Table 4.2).

Table 4.2   Score Table for GPM Goals

GPM % ACHIEVED	SCORE (POINTS)
46% AND ABOVE	200
45%	190
44%	180
43%	170
42%	160
41%	150
40%	140
39%	130
38%	120
37%	110
36% (HISTORICAL AVERAGE)	100
35%	80
34%	60
33%	40
32%	20
LESS THAN 32%	0

Threshold = 32, Ceiling = 46%, Increment = 1%

5.   WEIGHT ALLOCATION OF INCENTIVE FACTORS TO SM

Job Description	Factor Weight Allocation (F)		
	Sales (F1)	GPM (F2)	Orders (F3)
Sales Manager	40%	20%	40%

6.   COMMISSION CALCULATION METHOD

The SM score in each incentive factor category is multiplied by the factor weight allocated to it and divided by 100 percent. Adding all category scores times their factor weight yields the commission multiplier (CM).

If the SM achieves a combined score of more than 100 points his commission will be higher.

The commission multiplier is derived using the following formula:

$$\text{CM (Commission Multiplier)} = \frac{S1 \times F1}{100} + \frac{S2 \times F2}{100} + \frac{S3 \times F3}{100}$$

Where S1, S2, S3 are scores achieved for the incentive factors and F1, F2, F3 are weights allocated to each factor respectively. Note that F1+F2+F3 = 100%.

The final monthly commission is calculated as follows:

$$\text{MC (Monthly Commission)} = \text{CM (Commission Multiplier)} \times \text{CP (Compensation Pie)}$$

Where:

$$\text{CP} = \text{GP\$} \times \text{CA}$$

GP\$ = Gross profit dollars earned

CA = Commission Allocated to SM is 1% of GP\$ earned

The compensation pie for SM will be:

Compensation Source	Compensation Allocation
Gross Profit Dollars Earned (GP$)	1%

SM will receive a monthly bonus statement per attached example.

The company reserves the right to make changes or adjustments to this commission plan without any notice.

7.   EXAMPLE OF MONTHLY COMMISSION CALCULATION

7.1   Incentive Factors Actual Results

For the month of December 1999 the following results were gathered after the end of the month for the incentive factors allocated to the sales manager:

December 1999

Incentive Factor	Goal	Actual	% Achieved	Score (S)	Factor (F)	S x F
Sales	1.0 M	1.1 M	110%	120	40%	48
GPM	36%	38	_____	120	20%	24
Booking	1.1 M	1.2 M	109%	110	40%	44
Total Score						116
CM (Commission Multiplier)	116 / 100 =					1.16

7.2   Compensation Source Actual Results

The following result was reported for gross profit dollars earned:

Compensation Source	Period 12/99	Allocation	Total
GP$	$300,000	1%	3,000
Total Compensation Source			3,000

7.3   Monthly Commission Calculation

MC	=	CM	x	CP
(Monthly Commission)		(Commision Multiplier)		(Compensation Pie)

MC   =   1.16 x 3,000 = $ 3,480

ABC CORP. INCENTIVE COMPENSATION PLAN FOR OFFICE MANAGER (OFM)

JANUARY 2000

CONFIDENTIAL

1. INTRODUCTION

This Incentive Compensation Plan is intended to provide the office manager (OFM) with a quarterly incentive pay based on the following four incentive factors:

1. Meeting the Corporation's Revenue Goals

2. Meeting the Corporation's Cost Reduction Goals

3. Performance Evaluation

4. Personal Objectives

Payments will be made within 30 days of the quarter ending date provided that the OFM was fully employed by ABC Corp. for the whole quarter.

2. PLAN PRINCIPLES

The plan will be operated on the following principles:

a) Set the Goals

The company will set the corporate and OFM's goals on an annual basis and revise them as needed.

b) Measure Performance

The company will measure its performance and the OFM's performance on a quarterly basis.

c) Reward

The company will reward the OFM on a quarterly basis depending on the measured results at the end of the compensation period.

3. PLAN STRUCTURE

3.1 The plan is based on the four incentive factors mentioned in Section 1 which have been determined as critical to the company's growth and profitability.

3.2 The OFM is designated a factor weight for each of the incentive factors assigned to his job function. The weight allocation depends on how important these factors are in achieving the goals. The total weight allocated for all incentive factors is 100 percent.

4. INCENTIVE FACTORS

The following incentive factors are used in the plan:

4.1 Corporate Revenue Goals

The corporate revenue goals are set at the beginning of every year. The revenue goals for ABC Corp. for fiscal year 2000 are shown in Table 4.1.1 below,

**Table 4.1.1 Revenue Goals for ABC Corp.
Fiscal Year 2000**

Period	Revenue $
Q1	2.425M
Q2	2.625M
Q3	2.600M
Q4	2.900M
Total	10.550M

The OFM role is instrumental in providing services and support functions to meet the revenue goals.

At the end of every quarter, *actual* revenues are compared to the goals and the percent of goal achieved is determined. A corresponding score is assigned to the level of percent of goals achieved. See Table 4.1.2 on *page 159*.

Table 4.1.2   Score Table for Revenue Goals

% OF GOAL ACHIEVED	SCORE (POINTS)
150% and above	175
145%	165
140%	160
135%	150
130%	145
125%	140
120%	130
115%	125
110%	120
105%	110
100%	100
95%	95
90%	90
85%	70
80%	50
LESS THAN 80%	0

Threshold = 80%, Ceiling = 150%, Increment = 5%

Example: % of Goals Achieved $= \dfrac{\text{Actual Revenue}}{\text{Revenue Goal}} = \dfrac{1.25M}{1.1M} = 113.6\%$

➢ 113% corresponds to a score of 120 points.

NOTE: For percentages that fall in between, refer to lower figures and scores (i.e., if 113% is achieved, refer to 110% and 120 score).

4.2   Cost Reduction Goals

Cost reduction goals are set at the beginning of the year for each functional unit or department. Cost reduction goals for the Administration department of ABC Corp. for the fiscal year 2000 are shown in Table 4.2.1:

Table 4.2.1 Cost Reduction Goals for Administration Department

Q1	Q2	Q3	Q4	Total
$ 20,000	$ 25,000	$ 30,000	$ 25,000	$ 100,000

The OFM will play a critical role in achieving the cost reduction goals of the Administration department.

At the end of the quarter, the *actual* cost reduction achieved is compared to the goal and a percent of goal achieved is determined. A corresponding score is assigned to the level of percent of goal achieved using the cost reduction score table shown below.

Table 4.2.2   Score Table for Cost Reduction Goal

COST REDUCTION % ACHIEVED	SCORE (POINTS)
150%	180
140%	160
130%	150
120%	140
110%	130
100%	110
90%	100
80%	90
70%	70
60%	50
50%	40
Below 50%	0

Threshold = 50, Ceiling = 150%, Increment = 10%

4.3   Performance Evaluation Goals

The performance evaluation criteria established for the OFM is shown in Table 4.3.1. The weight allocation indicates the importance each criterion plays in the OFM's performance of the job function.

Table 4.3.1   Performance Criteria and Allocated Weight for OFM

Performance Categories	*Weight Allocated*
Problem-solving	30%
Assertiveness	25%
Teamwork	25%
Efficiency	20%
Total Weight	**100%**

At the end of every quarter, the OFM's personal performance will be rated using the following rating system:

5 = Excellent

4 = Very good

3 = Acceptable

2 = Marginal

1 = Unacceptable

(0.5 increment can be used for in between scores, e.g. 2.5, 3.5, etc.). A score is assigned depending on the rating the OFM achieves. The performance evaluation score table is shown below.

Table 4.3.2 Performance Evaluation Score Table for OFM

Weighted-Rating	Score
Min 30	20
32	33
34	46
36	59
38	72
40	85
42	98
44	111
46	124
48	137
Max 50	150

Threshold = 30, Ceiling = 50, Increment = 2.0

NOTE: Maximum rating is 50, minimum rating is 30. A rating below 30 will nullify the portion of the incentive allocated to this factor.

4.4 Personal Objectives

The OFM will be assigned personal objectives on a quarterly basis. The objectives assigned to the OFM for the first quarter of the fiscal year 2000 are displayed in Table 4.4.1 on *page 162.*

Table 4.4.1   Personal Objectives Components

Employee Name: Office Manager			Period: Q1/2000	
Group: Administration				
Objective	Difficulty Level	Priority	Due Date	Weight
Prepare monthly financial reports for management review	8	1	1/30/2000	40%
Review and prioritize all departments expense reports	7	2	2/28/2000	30%
Maintain customer database	8	3	3/31/2000	30%
Total	24			100%

At the end of the period, each objective will be reviewed and a percentage completion will be assigned. Score table 4.4.2 will be used to define the achievement level expected from the OFM.

Higher levels of completion of the personal objectives will lead to higher scores.

Table 4.4.2   Personal Objectives Score Table

% of Completion		Score
(Min. expected)	80%	30
	85%	50
	90%	70
	95%	90
(Max.)	100%	100

Threshold = 80%, Ceiling = 100%, Increment = 5%

NOTE: If below 80% completion is obtained, the value of the incentive allocated to this factor will be nullified.

When the total difficulty level assigned to the OFM's personal objectives exceeds 20, the OFM score will be boosted using the following score adjustment table.

Table 4.4.3 Personal Objectives Score Adjustment Table

Total Difficulty Level	Score Adjustment %
20 (Min. Difficulty Level)	100%
22	110%
24	120%
26	130%
28	140%
30	150%

Threshold = 20, Ceiling = 30, Increment = 2

For example, if the OFM completed 100 percent of their tasks and their total difficulty level was 30, their score will be boosted to:

100	x	150%	=	150
(Original) Score)		(Score Adjustment)		(Boosted Score)

5. WEIGHT ALLOCATION OF INCENTIVE FACTORS TO OFM

Job Description	Factor Weight Allocation (F)			
	Revenue (F1)	Cost Reduction (F2)	Performance Evaluation (F3)	Personal Objectives (F4)
Office Manager	30%	30%	20%	20%

6. INCENTIVE PAY CALCULATION METHOD

The OFM score in each incentive factor category is multiplied by the factor weight allocated to it and divided by 100 percent. Adding all category scores times their factor weights yields the performance index (PI). If the OFM achieves a combined score of more than 100 points their bonus will be higher.

The performance index is derived using the following formula:

$$PI \text{ (Performance Index)} = \frac{S1 \times F1}{100} + \frac{S2 \times F2}{100} + \frac{S3 \times F3}{100} + \frac{S4 \times F4}{100}$$

Where S1, S2, S3, S4 are scores achieved for the incentive factors and F1, F2, F3, F4 are weights allocated to each factor respectively. Note that F1+F2+F3+F4 =100%.

The final quarterly bonus is calculated as follows:

QB	=	PI	x	CP
(Quarterly Bonus)		(Performance Index)		(Compensation Pie)

Where:

PI	=	Performance Index
CP	=	Compensation Pie.

The compensation pie for the OFM will consist of the following two elements:

Compensation Source	Allocation
Pre-tax Profits	0.30 %
Cost Reduction	5.0 %

OFM will receive a quarterly bonus statement per attached example.

The company reserves the right to make changes or adjustments to this incentive pay plan without any notice.

7.   EXAMPLE OF QUARTERLY BONUS CALCULALTION

7.1   Incentive Factors Actual Results

For the period of Q1/2000 the following results were reported for the incentive factors allocated to the office manager:

Period Q1/2000

Incentive Factor	Goal	Actual	% Achieved	Score (S)	Factor (F)	S x F
Total Revenue	2.425M	2.55M	105%	110	30%	33
Cost Reduction	20,000	22,500	112%	130	30%	39
Performance Evaluation	50	42		98	20%	19.6
Personal Objectives *	100%	95%	95%	108	20%	21.6
Total Score						113.2
PI (Performance Index)			113.2 / 100 =			1.132

*For personal objectives factor, the score for 95 percent completion is 90 and the score adjustment for a difficulty level of 24 is 120 percent.

The adjusted score for personal objectives is: 90 x 120% = 108

7.2   Compensation Source Actual Results

The following results were reported on the compensation sources:

Compensation Source	Q1/2000 Results	Allocation	Total
Pre-tax Profit	$ 250,000	0.30%	$ 750
Cost Reduction	$ 22,500	5%	$ 1,125
		Total Compensation Source	$ 1,875

7.3   Quarterly Bonus Calculation

QB	=	PI	X	CP
(Quarterly Bonus)		(Performance Index)		(Compensation (Pie)

QB   = 1.132 x 1,875 = $ 2,122.50

CHAPTER ELEVEN
REVIEW OF MOTIVATION THEORIES

11.1 Introduction
In this chapter we will review a number of current human motivational theories. These theories serve as the basis for designing and implementing incentive compensation plans for most organizations. This chapter will provide a brief review of the work done by several researchers and other authors in the field who have examined and summarized motivational theories.

11.2 Motivation Theories
Motivation theories can be arranged in two main categories: **Content theories** and **Process theories**.

Content theories focus on the forces and needs within a person that drive motivated behavior. Content theories shed light on the individual needs of people, their inner ability to maintain motivated behavior and what rewards they consider as fulfilling their needs. The theories of Maslow, McClelland, and Herzberg, which are considered the most prominent in the field, will be examined in section 11.3.

Process theories vary from content theories in that they attempt to provide an insight into the thought process of individuals, determining what makes them behave in certain ways. In section 11.4 we will discuss two process theories: the Equity Theory and the Expectancy Theory. These theories offer valuable application into management's ability to maintain a highly motivated workforce in today's competitive environment.

Content theories are focused on individual's needs and their satisfaction factors. Process theories are more related to the individual's work efforts and their impact on job performance.

Content and process motivation theories cover different aspects of motivated behavior. When they are used complementary to each other, they enable management to understand how they can motivate individuals to achieve high levels of performance and satisfaction.

11.3 Content Theories

11.3.1 Maslow's Hierarchy of Needs Theory

Maslow's Hierarchy of Needs Theory consists of two main segments:

    (i) *Higher Order Needs*: self-actualization and esteem;

    (ii) *Lower Order Needs:* social, safety, and physiological.

According to Maslow's theory, the lower order needs must be fulfilled in the sequence they are presented in Figure 11.3.1 before the higher order needs can be activated as motivators. The arrows to the right indicate the order in which needs must be met, from the bottom up. Therefore, the physiological needs must be fulfilled before the safety needs; the safety needs must be fulfilled before the social needs, and so on.

Figure 11.3.1 Maslow's Hierarchical Needs

HIGHER ORDER NEEDS

Self-Actualization
Highest need level; need to fulfill one's self; to grow and use abilities to fullest and most creative extent.

Esteem
Need for esteem of others; respect, prestige, recognition, need for self-esteem, personal sense of competence, mastery.

LOWER ORDER NEEDS

Social
Need for love, affection, sense of belonging, in relationships with other people.

Safety
Need for security, protection and stability in the physical and interpersonal events of day-to-day life.

Physiological
Basic human needs; biological maintenance; food, water, sex, etc.

168

11.3.2   McClelland's Acquired Needs Theory

In the late 1940s, the psychologist David L. McClelland used a unique method to investigate human's most important needs. He used a test called the Thematic Apperception Test (TAT) as a tool to extract information from participants in his experiments. The TAT asked individuals to view pictures and write stories about what they saw.

McClelland identified three needs that appeared consistently in the TAT stories. These needs are:

- *Need for Achievement* (nAch): The desire to do something better or more efficiently, to solve problems, or to master complex tasks.
- *Need for Affiliation* (nAff): The desire to establish and maintain friendly and warm relations with other persons.
- *Need for Power* (nPower): The desire to control other persons, to influence their behavior, to be responsible for other people.

McClelland concluded that people develop these three needs over time and as a result of their life experiences. Each need can act as a motivator and can be linked to the work environment or job function that individuals prefer. Managers who learn to identify the presence of nAch, nAff, and nPower in themselves and others can match these needs profiles to positions, job functions, and work environments so that employees can thrive and maximize their performance.

For example, a person with high nAch can be most effective in a sales position with challenging sales goals and a potential to earn substantial commissions. A person with high nAff can do very well in an administrative or technical support role, and a person with high nPower will seek a supervisory management position with responsibility over a department or a group of people.

11.3.3 Herzberg's Two-Factor Theory

Frederick Herzberg's research on motivation focused on asking workers two simple questions:

1. "Tell me about a time when you felt exceptionally good about your job."
2. "Tell me about a time when you felt exceptionally bad about your job."

After analyzing a few thousand responses, Herzberg concluded that workers divided their answers into two categories:

(i) elements that made them feel good about themselves and provided them with job satisfaction, hence called, **satisfiers,** and

(ii) elements that caused discontent, unhappiness and frustration, hence called, **dissatisfiers.**

Dissatisfiers

Dissatisfiers are associated with where people work and the environment in which they work. This means that job satisfaction is more influenced by a person's job setting than by the type of work or function they perform. Figure 11.3.4 shows a number of examples of dissatisfiers in work settings.

Figure 11.3.4   Dissatisfiers Found in Work Settings

Company Rules and Procedures	Attendance rules Vacation schedules Performance appraisal methods
Working Conditions	Noise levels Safety Personal comfort Size of work area
Interpersonal Relationships	Co-worker relations Customer relations Relationship with boss
Quality of Supervision	Ability of supervisor
Base Salary	Hourly wage rate

<u>Satisfiers or Motivators</u>

Herzberg concluded that improving a dissatisfying element such as personal comfort at work, would not cause employees to become satisfied with their job. It will only prevent them from being unhappy about a situation that was corrected.

In order to foster satisfaction within the workforce, strong motivational factors must be introduced. By adding motivational factors to people's jobs their performance can be maximized. Examples of motivational factors or satisfiers include: growth opportunities, promotions, recognition, responsibility, etc. According to Herzberg, in the absence of motivational opportunities to drive the workforce, employees will not be happy nor will they perform well.

11.4 Process Theories

11.4.1 Equity Theory

Equity theories focus on motivation from the perspective of the social comparison people make among themselves and others. While Needs Theories suggest that our behavior is most influenced by inner needs and drives, Equity Theory sees our behavior as influenced by a desire to achieve fair and equitable treatment relative to those around us.

Equity Theory distinguishes between two different ways people make comparisons among themselves and others — outcomes and inputs. *Outcomes* are those things that are the results or outcomes of work, such as pay, prestige, or fringe benefits. *Inputs* are the efforts required to produce the outcomes, such as hours worked, qualifications, and the degree of effort expended. Equity Theory predicts that people will become unhappy when they compare themselves with others and find that inputs or outputs don't match up fairly. For example, if a manufacturing firm adopted a pay structure that compensated newly hired staff with less pay (outputs) than their existing workforce for the same work (inputs), Equity Theory predicts that this structure will cause considerable motivational problems. Moreover, if the manufacturing firm hopes that the demotivating effect of this inequity will be short term and will go away once everyone gets used to the new system, Equity Theory predicts that the demotivating effect of the inequity will continue and have a devastating influence on long-term employee motivation.

Negative and Positive Inequities

Employees feel two types of inequities:

- Negative inequity occurs when individuals feel that while being more productive than others in the performance of the job (input) others were rewarded more than they (output).

- Positive inequity occurs when individuals feel that they were rewarded (outcome) more than their peers for the same amount of work (input).

When individuals feel either a negative or a positive inequity, they will attempt to behave in ways they perceive will correct the situation they are confronted with.

Some examples of behavior resulting from perceived negative inequity:
- Quit the job.
- Reduce work efforts.
- Request a pay increase.
- Delegate work to fellow employees.
- Steal from the employer.
- Engage in non-productive or counter-productive activities in the workplace.

Some examples of behavior resulting from perceived positive inequity:
- Increase work input.
- Increase performance levels.
- Improve quality of work.
- Improve skills and competencies.

The research is most conclusive in respect to negative inequity; it appears people are less comfortable when they are under-rewarded than when they are over-rewarded.

Job Satisfaction versus Rewards

When employees feel the rewards they receive are fair and equitable, their job satisfaction and performance increase. When employees feel the rewards they receive are unfair, however, they become demotivated, demoralized, and unproductive.

It is critical for management to be aware of any potential negative inequities in order to avoid the impact of behaviors associated with such comparisons. Before allocating rewards such as pay raises, promotions, bonuses, gifts, etc., managers and supervisors should consider that each employee might make an equity comparison.

Managers should interview all employees and communicate to them their assessment of the employee's performance, the evaluation categories used in the assessment, and how the reward was allocated. A standardized method of evaluation should be used when reviewing employee performance. This method should be communicated and explained to all employees at the beginning of the year so they understand how they are expected to perform. Each employee should be informed as to which performance categories will be used in his or her periodic evaluation. For each evaluation category a score will be assessed and the employee should have the opportunity to respond to the assessed score. This is the opportunity for inequities to surface and be resolved before the actual reward is allocated.

Managers should discuss the reward openly with employees and determine if they feel it's fair and sufficient for their efforts. Resolve any issues equitably and mutually rather than allowing a situation to develop in which the employees keep the problems to themselves and try to find their own solutions.

11.4.2 Expectancy Theory

Expectancy Theory's central question is: "What determines the willingness and drive of an individual to maximize their personal effort to perform jobs that contribute to the productivity of their workgroup and the entire organization?"

The best-known Expectancy theories are those of Vroom, Porter and Lawler. Expectancy Theory states that people are motivated to work when they expect they will be able to achieve their goals in life through their jobs. The three major concepts underlying Expectancy Theory are:

1. **Expectancy (E)**, the individual's belief about the relationship between his or her efforts and performance.
2. **Instrumentality (I)**, the individual's belief about the relationship between his or her performance and the desired outcome.
3. **Valence (V)**, the amount of satisfaction an individual believes he or she will obtain of a given outcome.

Vroom developed the following equation to demonstrate the relationship among the key terms in the theory: Motivation (M), Expectancy (E), Instrumentality (I), and Valence (V)

$$M = E \times I \times V$$

This equation indicates that whenever one of the motivational elements (E, I, or V) is reduced, the motivational state of a person can be significantly lowered. Management should pay close attention to these three factors and try to keep them at high levels in order to foster positive attitudes among employees, maximizing performance.

Work Setting Applications

The challenge for managers is to create a work environment that combines organizational growth with the need for individuals to achieve personal long-term goals.
Note that employee surveys can act as valuable tools to extract information from the workforce prior to setting rewards and recognition programs in the organization.

Figure 11.4.2 on *page 175* summarizes real work applications of Expectancy Theory.

Figure 11.4.2 How should Managers use Expectancy Theory

EXPECTANCY FACTOR	WHAT THE EMPLOYEE WILL ASK	WHAT THE MANAGER SHOULD DO
Expectancy	"Is it realistic for me to achieve the desired level of performance?"	Select employees qualified for the job Train employees to use their abilities to do the job Utilize organizational resources to support employees' efforts Set clear performance goals Set clear performance criteria
Instrumentality	"What work outcomes and rewards will I receive as a result of the performance?"	Set clear performance versus rewards criteria Communicate performance and goal attainment progress periodically Clearly define rewards Clarify that rewards are contingent upon acceptable performance levels
Valence	"What value do I attach to the work outcome?"	Find out what rewards are considered of high value by employees Provide a large selection of rewards to match diversified needs Provide rewards of retainable memorable value that link employee to the organization.

11.5 Individual Performance Factors

There are three key elements that must be considered when attempting to influence individual performance. They can be expressed in the following equation:

$$\text{Performance} = \text{Individual Abilities} \times \text{Expended Effort} \times \text{Support System}$$

This equation views performance as the result of:

a. The personal skills and competency of individuals, that is their capability to perform,

b. The amount of energy they expend in doing their job, that is their willingness to perform, and

c. The organizational support in terms of facilitating tools, equipment, supplies, budgets, etc., which provides them with the opportunity to perform.

Since the three factors are multiplied by each other, and not added, all three must be present for high performance levels to be achieved. Each factor should be maximized for every individual on the workforce in order to maximize performance on the individual, group, and organizational levels. Managers need to be educated and trained to recognize and understand how each factor, acting alone and in combination with others, can have an impact in performance.

Motivation describes the internal drives within an individual that account for the amount, direction, and persistence of *effort* put forth toward the job. An employee who is highly motivated works hard. In order to reach high performance levels, however, an employee will need the other two components in the formula, their individual skills and the continuous support and encouragement of the organization.

11.6 Conclusions

Both content and process theories contribute in their own way to our understanding of how to generate motivation and drive performance. Using elements from each theory and applying them to the needs identified in each organizational setting, an effective motivational program can be put in place to promote employee morale, foster loyalty, and enhance performance.

We have learned that performance is dependent on three major elements:

In order to maximize work efforts, companies need to create a motivational atmosphere to drive their workforce.

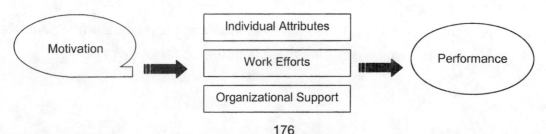

This is accomplished by allocating rewards that are contingent upon goal attainment.

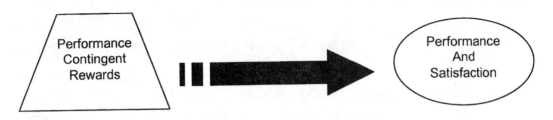

Researchers Porter and Lawler integrated the various theories into a model of individual performance and satisfaction. See Figure 11.6

Figure 11.6   Model of Individual Performance and Satisfaction

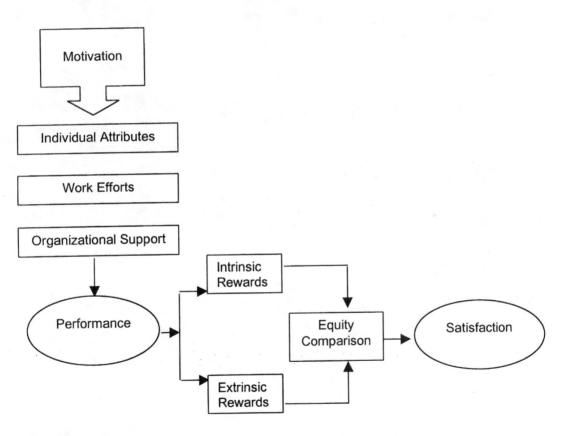

In addition, we can identify the following elements as critical in the foundation of any incentive compensation plan in the workplace:

(a) Realistic and attainable goals need to be set to drive the performance of the work force.

(b) The organizational goals and performance criteria need to be well defined and communicated to all employees in order to provide guidance and direction as to the expected results.

(c) Valuable award tools must be defined and made available to reward employees for achieving the desired objectives. In other words, employees should know what rewards they will receive for each level of performance accomplished.

(d) Organizations must provide the tools and support to facilitate the ability to succeed.

APPENDIX I

START YOUR INCENTIVE PLAN NOW

This appendix will help you design your incentive compensation plan. The attached eight instruction sheets will guide you through the initial design and setup process. Follow these steps to determine the critical elements that will be the building blocks for your incentive plan.

Each step has two parts:
1. The **Setup Step** is an example based on a sample company created using the organizational chart shown in Exhibit A on page 180;
2. The **Worksheet** is a form provided for your use. Fill it out based on your organizational structure and the specific requirements of your incentive compensation plan.

You may need to make several copies of the worksheets before you start to allow sufficient space to enter data and make modifications. These worksheets are also available at our Website www.incensoft.com/worksheets.htm. You can download them, complete and edit them as needed.

Upon completion of the eight worksheets, you may forward them to sales@incensoft.com (Subject: Worksheets) or fax them to Fax# 240-631-2804. Based on the information you provide, an IncenSoft Program Consultant will contact you to assist you in building an operational incentive plan tailored specifically for your organization.

Exhibit A

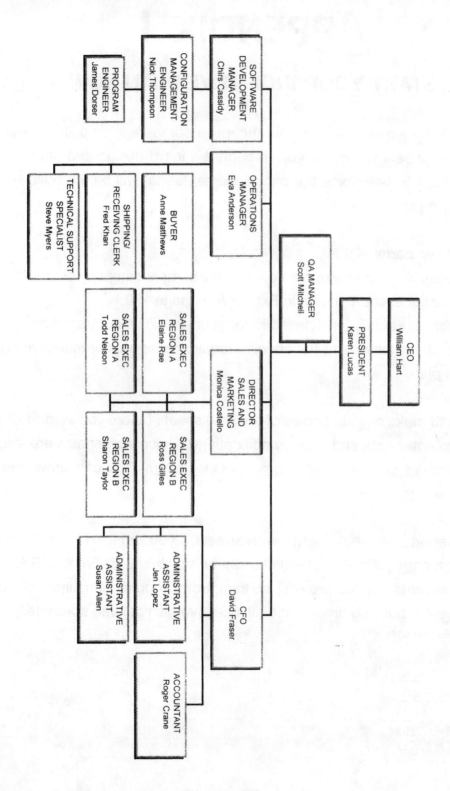

Setup Step #1: Set the Strategic Corporate Goals

- These goals should reflect the company's aspirations and long-term strategic plans.
- Goals should preferably be presented in a three to five-year time frame.
- Goals must be realistic, attainable, and well communicated to all employees involved in the incentive plan. <u>See example below.</u>
- Refer to Chapter 2, section 2.3, *Setting the Corporate Goals,* for complete information.

Corporate Goals	Current Year	Year 1	Year 2	Year 3
Sales Dollars	4.5M	5.0M	6.0M	7.0M
Improve Gross Profit Margin	34%	36%	38%	40%
Pre-Tax Earnings	400K	500K	625K	750K
Reduce Cost	N/A	50K	75K	100K
Release of New Product	2	4	5	6
Control Budget	1.0M	1.2M	1.4M	1.6M
Improve Customer Satisfaction	85%	90%	93%	96%
Achieve Booking of Orders	5.0M	5.5M	7.0M	8.0M
Earnings Per Share	$ .25	$ .30	$ .35	$ .45
Noncompliance in ISO9000 Audit	3	2	1	0
Other Examples of Goals				
EBIT				
Economic Value Added (EVA)				
Gross Profit Dollars Earned				
Increase in Profits				
Increase in Sales Dollars				
Net Income				
Number of Units manufactured				
Return on Capital				
Return on Investment				
Number of Units Shipped				
Total Revenue				
Total Stockholder Return				
Reduce A/R Collection Cycle				

Worksheet #1: Set the Strategic Corporate Goals

- Enter your corporate goals in this worksheet.
- These goals should reflect the company's aspirations and long-term strategic plans.
- Goals should preferably be presented in a three to five-year time frame.
- Goals must be realistic, attainable, and well communicated to all employees involved in the incentive plan.

You may edit this worksheet to reflect your corporate goals

Corporate Goals	Current Year	Year 1	Year 2	Year 3

Setup Step #2: Identify Groups and Subgroups

- Arrange all of the plan participants in a group and subgroup according to the organizational chart.
- Groups should be of similar job function and subject to similar work conditions (for example, a business unit, a corporate functional unit, a project team, etc).
- A subgroup may be an individual (i.e. VP of Administration) or several employees performing similar jobs (i.e. QA Inspectors). <u>See example below.</u>
- Refer to Chapter 2, section 2.4, *Setting the Organizational Structure,* for complete information.

Group	Subgroup	# of Employees
Executive (3)	CEO	1
	President	1
	QA Manager	1
Software Development (3)	Software Development Manager	1
	Configuration Management Engineer	1
	Program Engineer	1
Operations (4)	Operations Manager	1
	Buyer	1
	Shipping/ Receiving Clerk	1
	Technical Support Specialist	1
Sales and Marketing (5)	Director Sales and Marketing	1
	Sales Exec. Region A	2
	Sales Exec. Region B	2
Finance / Administration (4)	CFO	1
	Administrative Assistant	2
	Accountant	1
	Total Number of Employee in the Plan	19

Worksheet #2: Identify Groups and Subgroups

- Use this worksheet to create your organization's structure.
- Arrange all of the plan participants in a group and subgroup according to the organizational chart.
- Groups should be of similar job function and subject to similar work conditions (for example, a business unit, a corporate functional unit, a project team, etc).
- A subgroup may be an individual (i.e. VP of Administration) or several employees performing similar jobs (i.e. QA Inspectors).

Group	Subgroup	# of Employees
	Total Number of Employee in the Plan	

Setup Step #3: Determine and Assign Incentive Factors

- Incentive factors are the elements through which the organization can achieve its long-term strategic goals. They are the driving force to motivate and encourage employees to reach and exceed the established goals.
- Incentive factors can be selected from the business goals identified in Step 1.
- Incentive factors must be measurable using quantitative methods.
- Each group should be assigned the incentive factors for which they have responsibility and control. <u>See example below.</u>

Incentive Factors	Executive	Software Develop.	Operations	Sales & Mktg.	Finance / Admin
Sales Dollars	√	√		√	
GPM (%)	√			√	
Cost Reduction			√		√
New Product Develop.	√	√	√		
Budget	√	√	√	√	√
Customer Satisfaction	√	√	√	√	√
Employee Performance			√		√
Personal Objectives		√	√	√	√

In addition to the quantifiable incentive factors, the program allows you to select "Employee Performance" and "Personal Objectives" factors, which are optional.

- Refer to Chapter 3, sections 3.4, *Determining Incentive Factors*; and 3.5, *Assigning Incentive Factors to Groups*, for complete information.

Worksheet #3: Determine and Assign Incentive Factors

- Incentive factors are the elements through which the organization can achieve its long-term strategic goals. They are the driving force to motivate and encourage employees to reach and exceed the established goals.
- Incentive factors can be selected from the business goals identified in Step 1.
- Incentive factors must be measurable using quantitative methods.
- Each group should be assigned the incentive factors for which they have responsibility and control.

In addition to the quantifiable incentive factors, the program allows you to select "Employee Performance" and "Personal Objectives" factors, which are optional.

You may edit this worksheet to reflect your incentive factors as needed.

Incentive Factors	Group A	Group B	Group C	Group D	Group E
Employee Performance					
Personal Objectives					

Setup Step #4: Allocate Incentive Factor Weight to Subgroups

- Examine each subgroup and determine which factors should be the focus of their effort. Allocate a weight among the factors assigned to each subgroup. The total factor weight should equal 100 percent for each subgroup.
- Three groups are illustrated in this example.

Incentive Factors	Group : Executive		
	CEO	President	QA Manager
Sales Dollars	30	40	25
GPM (%)	20	20	--
New Product Develop.	25	20	25
Budget	10	--	25
Customer Satisfaction	15	20	25
Total Weight per Subgroup	100%	100%	100%

Incentive Factors	Group : Operations			
	Operations Mgr.	Buyer	Shipping/ Rec. Clerk	Tech. Support Sp.
Sales Dollars	25	--	50	30
GPM (%)	25	25	--	15
Cost Reduction	25	50	20	25
Budget	25	--	--	15
Performance Evaluation	--	--	15	15
Personal Objectives	--	25	15	--
Total Weight per Subgroup	100%	100%	100%	100%

Incentive Factors	Group : Software Development		
	Software Develop. Mgr.	Config. Mgmt. Eng.	Program Eng.
Sales Dollars	30	25	30
New Product Develop.	50	45	50
Budget	10	10	10
Customer Satisfaction	10	10	--
Personal Objectives	--	10	10
Total Weight per Subgroup	100%	100%	100%

- Refer to Chapter 3, section 3.6, *Allocating Incentive Factors and Weights to Subgroups*, for complete information.

Worksheet #4: Allocate Incentive Factor Weight to Subgroups

- Examine each subgroup and determine which factors should be the focus of their effort.
- A weight is distributed among the factors assigned to each subgroup. The total factors weight should equal 100 percent for each subgroup.

You may edit this worksheet to reflect the factor weights in your incentive plan as needed.

Group :				
Incentive Factors	Subgroup 1	Subgroup 2	Subgroup 3	Subgroup 4
Total Weight per Subgroup	100%	100%	100%	100%

Group :			
Incentive Factors	Subgroup 1	Subgroup 2	Subgroup 3
Total Weight per Subgroup	100%	100%	100%

Group :			
Incentive Factors	Subgroup 1	Subgroup 2	Subgroup 3
Total Weight per Subgroup	100%	100%	100%

Setup Step #5: Determine the Compensation Schedule

- Determine the appropriate compensation schedule for each group. At the end of each period, comparing the incentive factor goals to the actual performance results will determine the compensation pay.
- Compensation schedules may be bi-weekly, monthly, quarterly, semiannually or annually. <u>See example below.</u>

	Compensation Schedule			
Groups	Monthly	Quarterly	Semi-annually	Annually
Executive			√	
Engineering		√		
Operations		√		
Sales & Marketing	√			
Finance/Admin		√		

- Refer to Chapter 3, section 3.7, *Determining the Compensation Schedule*, for complete information.

Worksheet #5: Determine the Compensation Schedule

- Determine the appropriate compensation schedule for each group. At the end of each period, comparing the incentive factor goals to the actual performance results will determine the compensation pay.
- Compensation schedules may be bi-weekly, monthly, quarterly, semiannually or annually.

You may edit this worksheet to reflect the compensation schedule in your incentive plan as needed.

Groups	Compensation Schedule			
	Monthly	Quarterly	Semi-annually	Annually

Setup Step #6: Determine the Compensation Sources

- Select the financial resources that will fund your incentive plan. Your plan may be funded by a single or multiple compensation sources. Limit to three to four sources.
- Include projections for each compensation source (goals). <u>See example below.</u>

Compensation Source	Projected Source Revenue	Percent Allocated to the Plan	Projected Source Allocation *
Pre-Tax Profit	500K	20%	$ 100,000
Earnings per Share	.30	--	
Budget Surplus	250K	50%	$ 125,000
Cost Reduction	50K	50%	$ 25,000
		Total Projected Source Allocation	$ 250,000

Other Examples of Compensation Source		
Increase in Profits		
Percent of Salary		
Gross Profit $ Earned		
Increase in Sales $		
Net Income		
Total Revenue		
Return on Investment		
Return on Capital		

* **Projected Source Allocation = Projected Source Revenue X Percent Allocation**

- Refer to Chapter 3, section 3.9, *Selecting Compensation Sources,* for complete information.

Worksheet #6: Determine the Compensation Sources

- Select the financial resources that will fund your incentive plan. Your plan may be funded by a single or multiple compensation sources. Limit to three to four sources.
- Include projections for each compensation source (goals).

You may edit this worksheet to reflect the compensation sources in your plan as needed.

Compensation Source	Projected Source Revenue	Percent Allocated to the Plan	Projected Source Allocation *
Total Projected Source Allocation			

* **Projected Source Allocation = Projected Source Revenue X Percent Allocation**

Setup Step #7: Distribute the Compensation Sources

- First, distribute a percentage of each compensation source as assigned to each group.
- Further subdivide the percent of each compensation source allocated to the group, to the subgroup level.
- Repeat this step for every compensation source in your incentive plan.
- The example below illustrates the allocation of Pre-Tax Profit to groups and subgroups.

Compensation Source: Pre-Tax Profit					
Group	Sub-Group	# of Employees in Subgroup	% of Profit Allocation per Employee	% of Profit Allocation per Subgroup	% of Profit Allocation per Group
Executive	CEO	1	1.5	1.5	3.75
	President	1	1.5	1.5	
	QA Manager	1	.75	.75	
Engineering	Software Develop. Mgr.	1	75	.75	1.75
	Config. Mgmt. Engineer	1	.5	.5	
	Program Engineer	1	.5	.5	
Operations	Operations Manager	1	75	.75	2.05
	Technical Support Spec.	1	.5	.5	
	Shipping/Receiving Clerk	1	.4	.4	
	Buyer	1	.4	.4	
Sales & Marketing	Director, Sales & Mktg.	1	1.2	1.2	4.2
	Sales Executive, Region A	2	.75	1.5	
	Sales Executive, Region B	2	75	1.5	
Finance/ Admin.	CFO	1	1.5	1.5	2.8
	Administrative Assistant	2	.4	.8	
	Accountant	1	.5	.5	
	Number of Employees: 19			Total Profit Allocation:	14.55%

- Refer to Chapter 3, section 3.10, *Allocating Compensation Sources*, for complete information.

Worksheet #7: Distribute the Compensation Sources

- First, distribute a percentage of each compensation source as assigned to each group.
- Further subdivide the percent of each compensation source allocated to the group, to the subgroup level.
- Repeat this step for every compensation source in your incentive plan.

   You may edit this worksheet to reflect your incentive plan and add to it as needed.

Compensation Source:					
Group	Sub-Group	# of Employees in Subgroup	% of Profit Allocation per Employee	% of Profit Allocation per Subgroup	% of Profit Allocation per Group
	Number of Employees:		Total Profit Allocation:		

Setup Step #8 Determine the Incentive Factor Goals

- Set the goals to be accomplished by each group for every incentive factor assigned to it during the compensation period scheduled for the group. <u>See example below</u>.

Executive	Factor Goals				
	Sales $	GPM (%)	New Product	Budget	Customer Satisfaction
1/1/01-6/30/01	2.0M	36%	2	120K	88%
7/1/01-12/31/01	3.0M	36%	2	120K	90%

Operations	Factor Goals			
	Cost Reduction	New Product	Budget	Customer Satisfaction
1/1/01-3/31/01	12.5K	1	100K	88%
4/1/01-6/30/01	12.5K	1	100K	88%
7/1/01-9/30/01	12.5K	1	120K	90%
10/1/01-12/31/01	12.5K	1	120K	90%

Sales and Marketing	Factor Goals			
	Sales $	GPM (%)	Budget	Customer Satisfaction
1/1/01-1/31/01	330K	36%	25K	88%
2/1/01-2/28/01	330K	36%	25K	88%
3/1/01-3/31/01	330K	36%	25K	88%
4/1/01-4/30/01	330K	36%	25K	88%
5/1/01-5/31/01	330K	36%	25K	88%
6/1/01-6/30/01	350K	36%	25K	88%
7/1/01-7/31/01	500K	36%	25K	90%
8/1/01-8/30/01	500K	36%	25K	90%
9/1/01-9/30/01	500K	36%	25K	90%
10/1/01-10/31/01	500K	36%	25K	90%
11/1/01-11/30/01	500K	36%	25K	90%
12/1/01-12/31/01	500K	36%	25K	90%

Worksheet #8: Determine the Incentive Factor Goals for Each Group

- Set the goals to be accomplished by each group for every incentive factor assigned to it during the compensation period scheduled for the group.

  You may edit this worksheet to reflect the factor goals in your incentive plan as needed.

Group:					
Compensation Period	Factor Goals				
	Factor 1	Factor 2	Factor 3	Factor 4	Factor 5

Group:				
Compensation Period	Factor Goals			
	Factor 1	Factor 2	Factor 3	Factor 4

Group:				
Compensation Period	Factor Goals			
	Factor 1	Factor 2	Factor 3	Factor 4